I A M  M A N

OTHER BOOKS BY LEE MARACLE

Bobbi Lee: Indian Rebel
Sojourner's Truth and Other Stories
Sundogs
Ravensong
Telling It: Women and Language Across Cultures (co-editor)
Sojourners and Sundogs
Bent Box
Daughters are Forever

I AM WOMAN

A NATIVE PERSPECTIVE
ON SOCIOLOGY
AND FEMINISM

LEE MARACLE

PRESS GANG
AN IMPRINT OF RAINCOAST BOOKS

The Publisher acknowledges the ongoing financial support of the Government of Canada through The Canada Council for the Arts and the Book Publishing Industry Development Program (BPIDP); and the Government of British Columbia through the BC Arts Council.

Design by Val Speidel

NATIONAL LIBRARY OF CANADA CATALOGUING IN PUBLICATION DATA

Maracle, Lee 1950–
I am woman

ISBN 0-88974-059-3

Maracle, Lee 1950– 2. Indian women — British Columbia — Biography
Indian women — British Columbia — Social conditions. I. Title.
E78.B9M36 1996   305.4'88970711   C96-9102191-7

Press Gang Publishers   *In the United States:*
an imprint of Raincoast Books   Publishers Group West
2440 Viking Way   1700 Fourth Street
Richmond, British Columbia   Berkeley, California
Canada V6V 1N2   94710
www.raincoast.com

Printed in Canada.

10 9 8 7

CONTENTS

Preface to the Second Edition

THIS BOOK HAS been out of print for some years now. However, many people still seek it out, and eight years after its original publication it remains relevant. It is reproduced here under new cover and with some revisions, more to fill in gaps than to alter the original. *I Am Woman* represents my personal struggle with womanhood, culture, traditional spiritual beliefs and political sovereignty, written during a time when this struggle was not over. I had settled on very little when I first wrote *I Am Woman*, except this: I and other Native women ought to come by our perceptions of spirituality, culture, womanhood and sovereignty from a place free of sexist and racist influence. My point of view is presented in poetry and stories, and couched not so carefully in essays. My original intention was to empower Native women to take to heart their own personal struggle for Native feminist being. The changes to the text are to clarify meaning; they do not alter its original intention. It still remains my attempt to present a Native woman's sociological perspective on the impacts of colonialism on us, as women, and on myself personally.

I Am Woman was intended to release me from the chains with which I bound myself, chains which were welded to me by a history neither I nor my ancestors created. Bondage is paralyzing and removing chains is painful. When the chains are bound to you by internal attitudes and beliefs created by external world conditions, removing them is both painful and humbling. The text is an emotional one, free of the humour and joy that punctuated the struggle for being which this book represents. I do not apologize for that.

I am still humbled by my youthful enthusiasm which was crushed by the realization of the depth and extent of racial, sexist and nationalist oppression visited upon Native women. I am humbled by the absolute heroism required of the young mother that I was, wrestling with the conditions into which I was born. We are an internally colonized people. I am amazed at the number of victories I achieved under appalling conditions.

I was born during the 1950s to a mother who struggled relentlessly to feed, clothe and house eight children, instill in them some fundamental principles of culture, educate them in our original sense of logic and story and ensure they would still be able to function in the larger world. Although she was not entirely successful at feeding us on a regular basis, nor was she successful at mothering us consistently in the way that children need, she managed to re-create in me a deep sense of hope for the future, as well as national pride, social conscience, fairness and a tenacious will. Our mother insisted that those who eat must work, those who work are entitled to participate in the general management of the family and those who participate must be prepared to make intelligent choices about their life and family context. I matured early, worked hard my entire life and was granted access to some of the most intelligent people.

I trotted about with my mother to the homes of great intellectuals among the Squamish people, the nation from which my father hails. Among them were Andy Paull, a statesman and British Columbia's first constitutional lawyer, and his son, Percy,

I AM WOMAN

1. *I Want to Write*

SCRIBBLE ... SCRIBBLE ... scribble ... I gathered up a host of paper napkins, brown bags and other deadwood paraphernalia on which I had scribbled the stories that people gave me. Scribbled sitting in the back of buses, inside grungy restaurants and in the audiences of great gatherings. Typed out the scribbles between the demands of young children and worked them up for publication until finally they made their way to the printer.

On all these scraps are written the stories of people of my passion. In the early years of my political activism the passion expressed itself as a virulent hatred for the system which destroyed our lives, our families; today, the passion expresses itself as deep caring. I resisted publishing for a long time, not because I lacked confidence in the words scribbled on my scraps of paper—the voices of the unheard cannot help but be of value—but how can one squeeze one's loved ones small, onto the pages of a three-dimensional rectangle, empty of their form, minus their favourite colours and the rhythm of the music that moves them?

Not all the stories made it into this book, but the essence of them did. Some of the stories were from men—very few. Most were from the women and children who have waltzed in and out of my life. Through all of the stories runs a common thread: for us racism is not an ideology in the abstract, but a very real and practical part of our lives. The pain, the effect, the shame are tangible, measurable and murderous.

For those of us who would mumble uncomfortably, "It can't be all that bad," whisper that overtop the graves of the thirty-seven young people who began the Native youth and power movement of the 1960s. Most of the youth who perished were men. Young men in their prime. Men not yet fathers, and we shall never know their children; their lineage also is dead. They died suddenly, violently, though sudden death was not the only way to perish. Many young men simply disappeared. I used to wonder what happened to all the men who left the women I knew. Where did they go? I knew what happened to the women, but I never heard from the men.

The nagging and persistent clouds of this city draped her in a canopy of grey the day I walked through skid row, nostalgia overcoming me. The spring of 1980 fell upon me drearily. On East Hastings and Main Street, I discovered some of the missing men. Native men far outnumber Native women on "the drag." We have achieved an ironic modicum of equality on skid row. White men far outnumber their own women on that row too.

They die there—eventually. The average survival span on "the drag" is about five years. Alcoholism is still the biggest killer. It is not the polite alcoholism of the middle-class person who loses his home, his car or his job and finds his way to a treatment centre. "Bottoming out" for the middle class is the top of the ladder for the Native alcoholic. On the "skids" of the nation, alcoholism begins with Chinese cooking wine and ends with Lysol, canned heat, madness and a horrible death. It is all about passing out in a square where even the pigeons crap on you. It is all about falling asleep forever in a dumpster and being chewed up by the truck before you get to the dump.

My Gawd. Ol' Edmonds is still in the dumpster! From your sky-perch above Pigeon Square did your spirit see the confusion of legs, arms and shouts trying to stop the truck? Did you see the look of unspeakable horror twist the young white boy's face when he saw what he had done?

I have been told that, statistically, white males predominate on skid row. There are twice as many white as Native men there. That, my friends, is still way out of line for us. We are less than one-tenth of the population and we account for one-third of skid row. The fate of Native men, however, is the subject of another book, a book that will be written by a man who needs to become whole.

It is the practice of many writers to fictionalize reality and prostitute their fantasies. "Artistic licence," they call it (whoever "they" are). I, too, have taken the stories of my life and others' lives and added some pure fabrications of my imagination, rewriting them as my own.

Rather than distorting the facts, I have altered their presentation. They are presented as I saw them, from my own emotional, spiritual and visual perspective. To be faithful to my view I have put myself as the central figure in all the lives recounted here. If I was not really there, it does not matter. I have eyes and I can see.

Usually when one writes of oneself it is called nonfiction. I disbelieve that. Hindsight is always slightly fictitious. The events that shaped my life are written down here. They happened. They taught me the great lessons that altered the course of my life. They moved me to see that through all the hurt and the anger written into the lives of Native people, great love has survived. This love for many of us has been kept under lock and

key, waiting for the moment when its expression will meet a
humanistic response, but it is still there. I am continually surprised that so few of us are murderers.

From around the kitchen tables of the people I have known
have come stories of the heart. Great trust and love were
required to enable the bearer to part with the tale. If I wrote for
a lifetime I could never re-tell all the stories that people have
given me. I am not sure what to do with that, except that I shall
try to grasp the essence of our lives and to help weave a new
story. A story in which pain is not our way of life.

Poetry of a Girl-Child

Bright red sunrise
happy birds
with graceful wings
amid fluffy clouds

Let my life be filled with joy
and only punctuated by pain.

To the family of the grandmother whose teaching I combined with the teaching of another family's grandmother, who
insisted that I also call her grandmother, I apologize. The grandmother in this book, like Rusty, is a composite of a number of
old Native women I have known. Their lives, likewise, are a
composite of the reality of our history and present existence.
Their feelings about life are my own. Their teachings are
ancient and as closely accounted for as I can remember.

"If you live right the grandmothers will take care of you," I
was taught. Conversely, if you live wrong they will forsake you.
You will sicken and perhaps die. In 1979, I walked into a hospi-
tal a very sick lady. They strapped me to a strange bed and filled
my body with barbiturates. They tested me for this and that, but

couldn't figure out what was wrong. There was no doubt that something was seriously wrong.

The chief surgeon told me that I was dying of something, but they did not know what. I went home. I did not mind dying but I started to wish that I could have done more for my community. I wanted to finish bringing up my children in a safer and warmer world than the one I had endured. That was about when I started to live again.

I connected with Dennis at about this time. He knew that I was ill. It was a long time before we found out what was wrong and rectified it. Along with the physical treatment for my well-being there was love and Native spiritual and physical healing. I have the dubious honour of possessing the worst spinal sub-luxations ever treated by my chiropractor. What that lovely Latin teeth-sticking phrase translates into was daily and then thrice-weekly treatments to straighten out my back. It took two years. When I wrote that our "backs bent double with the effort" and "crippled and paralyzed us," I meant that figuratively and literally.

Love itself has the power to heal. To really appreciate and enjoy motherhood a woman must be loved. Unloved, she will invariably abuse or neglect her children in some way. The pain, effort and work of motherhood is rendered beautiful through her lover.

I love my children. They are my everything. I called them into being. I tried desperately to nurture and educate them. I learned to play again, to laugh at the moon and find pleasure in ladybugs and worms. But if I learned to laugh, sing, dance and be merry through my children, I also learned that they were temporary. You give them twenty years of your life, the best twenty years, and just when they get good at being people, they leave. My mother always said, "Take time out for yourself . . . take time out for your lover . . ." It really annoys a ten-year-old to think that she is not the centre of the universe—not even

your universe—but they do come to grips with it, provided
they have had a safe and loving upbringing. Just as I accept that
they are with us temporarily, so I learned that we are each but
one person in a long chain of people.

Creation

I know nothing
of great mysteries
know less of creation
I do know
that the farther backward
in time that I travel
the more grandmothers
and the farther forward
the more grandchildren
I am obligated to both.

I wanted to be a writer when I was still a "wharf rat" from
the mud flats. That was a long time ago. I did not want the
"fame" that went with it. The result of being colonized is the
internalization of the need to remain invisible. The colonizers
erase you, not easily, but with shame and brutality. Eventually
you want to stay that way. Being a writer is getting up there and
writing yourself onto everyone's blackboard. I did not know
that at first, and when I found I out I beat a hasty retreat for
some thirteen years. It was not my intention to get out there
and be visible when I was scribbling the words which would
eventually become part of this book.

I don't remember how Cj found out that I wrote poetry.
When she asked me to read, I doubt very much that she knew
how hard it was going to be for me. She and my partner were
the only ones who knew that I wrote poetry; everyone else
thought of me as a political essayist and occasional story writer.

I have said things that I now have to live with. I have told the world my private aspirations, my dreams and the pain of my resistance. I laid myself at everyone's feet. I have very little self left that is private.

I read because Cj asked me to. But I have a very different reason to be glad that I said yes to Cj. Not the usual joy of recognition, but because a young fifteen-year-old girl showed me why I needed to stand up. At a public meeting against apartheid, she got up and talked about youth, Native youth and liberation. An eighteen-year-old young woman got up and spoke about Native solidarity with Black people in South Africa. By standing up and laying myself bare, I erased invisibility as a goal for the young Native women around me. My children refuse to be among the many Native people made invisible.

Writing when I should have been mothering humbled me to my own blinders. Children, I have learned, grow up best when not hindered by parental interference. If one waters a plant too much, the plant drowns and dies; likewise with children. I learned to trust that internal discipline works after my daughters were five and six years old, when I became too busy writing to cudgel them with useless and harmful instructions. I learned that the art of parenting is all about providing one's children with the best possible conditions in which they can grow. This lesson did not come to me as some heavenly revelation at the birth of my first child, but after a half-dozen years of very destructive parenting and the challenge my children themselves posed to me.

Prohibition, sanction and force, the hallmarks of North American parenting, don't work. Many parents are fooled by model behaviour in their children. They are not well behaved, the parents are well trained, vigilant, and likely the children are terrified. But they grow up and, as teenagers, they realize in their new woman and man bodies the limits of parental force. We get old. Authority is lost. If a child was well behaved only because she was terrorized, she is apt to become one of the wild teenage problems that keep sociologists, police, parents and social workers so busy.

Poetry stripped my spirit of its bodily dress and prose removed the clothes with which I cloaked my character, but my children challenged my naked character and my spirit. They forced me to struggle to do as I say. They prepared me to follow them, not against Europeans, but alongside them, not contemptuous of their bias, but loving their ability to throw aside their own blinders and renounce their less-than-glorious present. Without children, I could not have learned that "everything is fixable."

Without children I could not have learned that what is revival and renaissance for a Native is death for a colonizer. For both of us there is re-construction and a future full of passion and compassion.

Without colonization, neither I nor my children would have had to suffer through the coming into being of this knowledge. Without colonization, there would not have been the need for "re-constructing" the passion and compassion we should naturally feel for one another. We, my children and I, should not have had to suffer to experience familial love.

Though I hold no animosity toward the Europeans in this land, I did not intend to write for them. My voice is for those who need to hear some truth. It has been a long time since I had an intimate discussion with my own people and those other people who are not offended by our private truth. It is inevitable that Europeans will read my work. If you do not find yourselves spoken to, it is not because I intend rudeness—you just don't concern me now.

There are those—both European and Native—who will be offended by the words in this book. It is not a friendly little fireside chat of the Mulroney variety. It does not focus on the so-called success stories in our community. It addresses Native people in desperate circumstances, those who need to recover the broken threads of their lives.

It is hard not to protest, not to address CanAmerican Europe when you are not just surrounded, but buried beneath the urban giant, reduced to a muffled voice by the twang and clang of machines. It is hard not to cry out to those next to you, "Come together . . . push up on the giant . . . bite his heels." It is easier to cry out to the unseen, deaf ears above for help.

Like miners in a shaft we are weighed down by the oppressive dirt which colonialism has heaped upon us. Unlike with miners, the dirt is heaped upon us deliberately and no one is terribly interested in removing the load—including ourselves.

Since "Uncle Willie" started giving us "hush money," we have stepped up the campaign against ourselves where the Europeans left off. We fight against each other with a fierceness we have not shown since our forefathers' early resistance. The anger inside has accumulated generation by generation, and because it was left to decay, it has become hatred. By its very nature, racism only permits the victimized race to engage that hatred among its own. Lateral violence among Native people is about our anti-colonial rage working itself out in an expression of hate for one another.

Hatred

If the State won't kill us
we will have to kill ourselves.

It is no longer good etiquette
      to head-hunt savages
we'll just have to do it ourselves.

It's not polite to violate "squaws"
      we'll have to find
an Indian to oblige us.

It's poor form to starve an Indian
    we will have to
deprive our young ourselves.

Blinded by niceties and polite liberality
    we can't see our enemy,
so, we'll just have to kill each other.

I would be cynical but for the tenacity of the late autumn
rose which stubbornly clings to life in a season when all flora is
laid to rest. The self-hate is not real. It is a cover for systemic
rage. The children I meet are the roses in autumn. Children are
forever blossoming. Their parents may feel crushed but the children go on blooming like the lovely, stubborn rose. Occasionally I meet adults who have reached deep inside the spirit of
themselves for the strength to bloom amid the death and
destruction just because they want to end it and I am inspired to
reach yet farther too.

Children are not far removed from the earth and they do not
mind digging. They are new, full of life and unable to be cynical. It is for them that I write the tragedy of our lives and the
truth of our emancipation. It is the children who will have to
learn to claw, dig and scratch in unison if we are to get out of
this deep shaft. The truth is that few miners caught in a shaft
ever dig themselves out.

The burden we carry is a collective one. Unfortunately, it is
in addition to the personal load that every human being carries.
Some of us have managed to deal quite adequately with our
personal lives and have fooled ourselves into thinking that seeing a light up above is enough.

The adage "Everything starts with the self" has some truth,
but it is not the whole truth. It is the basis for a person's passion,
but denies compassion. In figuring out a path for the whole
people, it must be borne in mind that the whole people may not
choose to forsake themselves.

"I succeeded on my own, why can't you?" is a dispassionate call to the majority of Native people to forsake one another. The end result is each of us digging our own way out of the hole, filling up the path with dirt as we go. Such things as justice and principles prevent the whole people from becoming dispassionate. Until all of us are free, the few who think they are remain tainted with enslavement.

2. *I Am Woman*

I USED TO consider myself a liberated woman. I woke up at the bottom of the mine shaft one morning, darkness above me, screaming, "I'm not like the rest . . . I'm not an alcoholic . . . a skid row bum . . . a stupid Native," ad nauseum. Each time I confronted white colonial society I had to convince them of my validity as a human being. It was the attempt to convince them that made me realize that I was still a slave.

It was this enslavement which moved me to retrace my own desertion. In these pages I recount the colour of traitorousness and my decision to reconnect myself to all of us struggling to remove the burden of a recent colonial history.

Striving

> I drank heartily of the settler's wine
> learned his language well;
> gazed with awe at his success

no pretty woman was I, nor
clever wit did possess

My striving went to naught
it was the trying
that shames me now.

Until March 1982, feminism, indeed womanhood itself, was
meaningless to me. Racist ideology had defined womanhood
for the Native woman as nonexistent, therefore neither the
woman question nor the European rebel's response held any
meaning for me. Ignorance is no crime. But when you trot your
ignorance before the world as though it were part of some profound truth, that is a crime.

I apologize to Robert Mendoza's wife and all the Native
women who watched the video that I made in San Francisco for
International Women's Day in 1978. You must have been personally offended by my denial of my own womanhood. I will
forever remember Robert's sensitive reply to my remark that it
was irrelevant that I was a woman. In a phone call in which he
praised my understanding of the colonial process, he added:
"Couldn't you see that perhaps it was because you were Native
and a woman that your insight was so powerful?"

His modest indignation sharpens the deep remorse I now feel
for those women who had to watch, red-faced, while this traitor blurted into a microphone, in front of a multitude of non-
Native women, that it mattered not that I was a Native woman.
"It was such a great video, a great presentation . . . Don't you
think that you could have taken responsibility for being a
woman and inspired our sisters, just a little, with the fact that
this incisive understanding that you have acquired was due, at
least in part, to the fact that you were a Native woman?" Robert
Mendoza pleaded into the phone from Pasmaquoddy, Maine.
And the words of my granny echoed in my ears . . . . "You will
remember what you need to know when the time comes."

(Ah, Robert, don't you see, I could not have done that, not then.)

Before 1961, we were "wards of the government," children in the eyes of the law. We objected and became, henceforth, people. Born of this objection was the Native question—the forerunner of Native self-government, the Native land question, etc. The woman question still did not exist for us. Not then.

I responded, like so many other women, as a person without sexuality. Native women do not even like the words "women's liberation" and even now it burns my back. How could I resist the reduction of women to sex objects when I had not been considered sexually desirable, even as an object? We have been the object of sexual release for white males whose appetites are too gross for their own delicate women.

Fishwife

I am unclean,
daughter of an unwashed,
    fisherwoman
    loud, lean and raw.

I have no manners
no finesse
    Iron will
    and loyalty
are all that I possess.

I am not a docile forest creature
a quaint curio
    I am a burning flame
    not yet uhuru
    not yet woman
but very much alive.

I woke up. I AM WOMAN! Not the woman on the billboard for whom physical work is damning, for whom nothingness, physical oblivion is idyllic. But a woman for whom mobility, muscular movement, physical prowess are equal to the sensuous pleasure of being alive. The dead alone do nothing. Paraplegics move. I want to move.

I want to look across the table in my own kitchen and see, in the brown eyes of the man who shares my life, the beauty of my own reflection. More. I want to look across my kitchen table at the women of colour who share my life and see the genius of their minds, uncluttered by white opinion. I want to sit with my grown daughters and experience the wonderment of our mutual affection. I want us to set the standard for judging our brilliance, our beauty and our passions.

Whereas Native men have been victims of the age-old racist remark "lazy drunken Indian," about Native women white folks ask, "Do they have feelings?" How many times do you hear from our own brothers, "Indian women don't whine and cry around, nag or complain." At least not "real" or "true" Indian women. Embodied in that kind of language is the negation of our femininity—the denial of our womanhood. And, let us admit it, beneath such a remark isn't there just a little coercion to behave and take without complaint whatever our brothers think "we have comin' "?

I used to believe such attempts at enforcing docility in women. Worse, I was convinced that love, passion/compassion were inventions of white folks. I believed that we never loved, wept, laughed or fought with each other. Divorce was unheard of. Did we then merely accept our wifely obligations to men the way a horse or an ox accepts yoke and bridle? I think not.

The denial of Native womanhood is the reduction of the whole people to a sub-human level. Animals beget animals. The dictates of patriarchy demand that beneath the Native male comes the Native female. The dictates of racism are that Native

men are beneath white women and Native females are not fit to
be referred to as women.

No one makes the mistake of referring to us as ordinary
women. White women invite us to speak if the issue is racism or
Native people. We are there to teach, to sensitize them or to
serve them in some way. We are expected to retain our position
well below them, as their servants. We are not, as a matter of
course, invited as an integral part of "their movement"—the
women's movement.

I am not now, nor am I likely to be, considered an authority
on women in general by the white women's movement in this
country. If I am asked to write, my topic is Native whatever, and
like as not, the request comes replete with an outline and the
do's and don'ts of what I may or may not say. Should I venture
out on my own and deal with women as a whole and not in
segregated Native fashion, the invitations stop coming.

I am not interested in gaining entry to the doors of the
"white women's movement." I would look just a little ridiculous sitting in their living rooms saying "we this and we that."
Besides, it is such a small movement. I say this for those Native
women who think that they may find equal relations among
white women and who think that there may be some solace to
be found in those relations.

We are slaves with our own consent. As women, we do not
support each other. We look at males when they speak and stare
off into space when a woman steps assertively into the breach of
leadership. Men who stand up and passionately articulate our
aspirations about sovereignty are revered as powerful leaders;
women who do so are "intimidating." We mock the liberation
of women. I too am guilty of acceding to the erasure of our
womanhood. I actually wrote articles with just the kind of stric-
tures that today sicken me. No more.

I used to be uncomfortable being with women. I can
remember saying to a close friend of mine that I had more men
friends than women. She nodded, yes, unoffended, but neither

of us could think of a single male to whom we could say the converse without offending his manhood. We both had become complicit in the erasure of ourselves as women, as Natives.

We have done enough to help Europeans wipe us off the face of the earth. Every day we trade our treasured women friends for the men in our lives. We even trade our sisters. Let Wounded Knee be the last time that they erased us from the world of the living. Let us all blossom beautiful and productive.

3. Isn't Love a Given?

I AM APPALLED by the fact that I have been asked on numerous occasions to state my position on the question of women and lesbianism. What really appalls me is that the person thinks that I ought to take a position on the sacred right of women to love and be loved. Isn't love a given?

But if I am appalled at being asked, I am doubly appalled and shamed by the fact that the question needs to be answered. We have not come a long way, baby. The prohibition of women's right to choose is all-encompassing in North America. It is the most deep-seated bias in the history of class society. Racism is recent; patriarchy is old.

Colonization for Native women signifies the absence of beauty, the negation of our sexuality. We are the females of the species: "Native," undesirable, non-sensuous beings that never go away. Our wombs bear fruit but are not sweet. For us intercourse is not marked by white, middle-class, patriarchal dominant-submissive tenderness. It is more a physical release from the pressure and pain of colonialism—mutual rape. Sex becomes one more of the horrors of enslavement, driving us to celibacy. The greater the intellectual paralysis, the more sex is required and the more celibacy is desired.

Does this seem incongruous? Yes, but so are paralysis and movement.

Our life is lived out schizophrenically. Our community desires emancipation. The greater the desire, the more surely do we leap like lemmings into the abyss of alcoholism, violence and suicide. We cannot see our enemy, but we know we must have one. We are standing at the precipice of national destruction.

Women kid themselves that traditionally we were this way or that way. In the name of tradition we consent to all kinds of oppressive behaviour from our men. How often have we stood in a circle, the only female Native, and our contributions to the goings-on are not acknowledged?—as though we were invisible. We are the majority of the membership of almost every Native organization at the lowest level, the least heard and never the leaders. It is not for want of our ability to articulate our goals or lead folks, either. We have been erased from the blackboard of our own lives.

What pains me is that I never saw this before. How often do we read in the newspaper about the death or murder of a Native man, and in the same paper about the victimization of a female Native, as though we were a species of sub-human animal life? A female horse, a female Native, but everyone else gets to be called a man or a woman. (I will qualify this by saying that I do not recall the death of a Black woman ever being reported. Gawd, Cj, let's hope it is because no Black woman ever died on skid row. But we know different, don't we?)

I have been to hundreds of meetings where the male members demand written submissions from female members while giving themselves the benefit of collective discussion and team development prior to any attempt to write it up, thus helping male speakers to sharpen their ideas. Worse, I have watched the chairperson sit and listen to an endless exchange between two male colleagues while a patient woman holds her hand in the air, waiting to be recognized.

It doesn't stop there. This anti-woman attitude by Native males seems to be reserved for Native women. The really big crime is that our men-folk rise when a white woman walks into the room. Native men go to great lengths to recognize her, and of course, where there is controversy, her word is very often the respected one.

We must and will have women leaders among us. Native women are going to raise the roof and decry the dirty house which patriarchy and racism have built on our backs. But first we must see ourselves as women: powerful, sensuous beings in need of compassion and tenderness.

Please bear with me while I try to unravel the tangled roots of this bias against love and choice. We must try to look at why women reject women's right to choose, and understand why women treat the love between women as some sort of leprous disease that is contagious. I cannot write for women who love women; so far, the only lovers in my life have been men. I *can* address the feelings of homophobia which preclude our ability to accept lesbians among us.

Homosexuality has been named abnormal. If love were a matter of mathematics, averages and so forth, then that would be a fitting way to look at it, since the majority of us are hetero-sexual. However, love is a thing of the spirit. It finds its major expression through the heart and body. Since contemporary society is based largely on the economics of class and power, norms and mathematics usually prevail. The nature of love, its spiritual, emotional and physical origins are never considered in the white, male point of view.

When men talk about love between people of the same sex as abnormal, they are not referring to love at all, but to sex. Since we are speaking about love, we will have to ignore the male viewpoint. When women refer to women who love women as unnatural, what they really mean—and this is pathetic—is that it is almost unheard of, and, they agree, it is not allowed. Men loving women is almost unheard of: does its scarceness make it abnormal, unnatural? Any love women can garner for themselves will appear unnatural if women are generally unloved.

Nowhere in the white, male conception of history has love been a motive for getting things done. That is unnatural. They can't see love as the force which could be used to move mountains, change history or judge the actions of people. Love/spirit is seen as a womanly thing and thus is scorned. Women love their sons but men influence, direct and control them. Women love their husbands; men provide for women in exchange for a stable home and conjugal rights and that ever-nurturing womanly love. Men scorn love. We are expected not only to accept this scorn in place of love, but to bear untold suffering at the hands of men. That there is violence in North American homes is taken for granted: "Everyone knocks the wife around once in a while." And does anyone want to admit that very often after a beating on a drunken Friday, a woman is expected to open up to further scorn by moaning and groaning happy sounds while the man who beat her helps himself to her body?

Have you ever heard a man honestly admit that a woman's fear, her surrendering as a result of having been intimidated, excites and arouses him? Rape, ladies and gentlemen, is commonplace in the home. In the home, it is not a crime. What is worse, in our desperate fear of being unloved, a good many women plead for mercy and accept responsibility for the beating and beg forgiveness for imaginary transgressions. Could this be where men get the idea that women "like it, ask for it" when the subject of rape is discussed?

To be quite frank, my friends, if that is how we feel about ourselves, then it is quite likely that we are going to be vitriolic about women who are not victimized in the same way. A woman who has found love apart from men is seen as a traitor just as a woman who has found the love of a gentle man is seen as undeserving. He, of course, must be a wimp—pussy-whipped. In our society it is loving women that is prohibited.

Sexuality is promoted as the end-all and be-all of woman-hood, yet perversely it is often a form of voluntary rape: self-deprecation and the transformation of women into vessels of biological release for men. Our bodies become vessels for male gratification, not the means by which we experience our own sexual wonderment. Any other sexuality is considered abnormal and to be derided. White women spend a lifetime striving for the beauty of large breasts, a small waist, clear skin and that practiced look of submissive stupidity that indicates they will quietly acquiesce to brutal sex.

A woman close to myself and my lover left her husband not too long ago. He beat her on a regular basis for some fifteen years. Between beatings, she told us that he would get on top of her and without ever looking at her, relieve himself of sexual tension. Over the years, she was never sure if, every time he had sex, she had volunteered herself up for rape. That is the kind of story I have heard over and over again just too frequently. It is the kind of sex that is going on in too many homes of the nation.

How many women on Saturday night face beer-breathed husbands in the darkness of their rooms, saying, "Please, no," to men who carry on without their consent? They don't scream because they would awaken their own children. Marriages end over a woman's right to say no in her own bedroom. The law says she must allow her husband conjugal rights. This amounts to reducing women's bodies to soft knots in deformed trees.

Divorce alone gives a woman the right to deny her husband rutting privileges on his terms. We certainly cannot go beating our husbands as they do us. We are not usually their physical equals. Before the shame of colonization caught up to us and our men-folk started behaving like lesser white men (the more brutish type), Native men used to respond to flirting from women. Some still do. We used to believe that men responded to women, naturally. We also believed that choice was sacred, and that women were sexually passionate beings. We had better get back to some of the traditions that kept us human.

Nearly every woman in North America, particularly if she is a woman of colour, knows the vacant look of a man who is "getting his rocks off," that phrase unspoken in polite company. Men say it to each other more often than anyone cares to face. The very thing we never bring up in mixed company is that basically men take great pride in referring to sex in just that way: "getting your rocks off," "changing your oil," etc. For those of you who think that feminism or women's liberation has brought about a change in this attitude, just go to a leftist social event and bring up the subject of fucking. There is no way to clear a room more quickly than to ask a man if he "got his rocks off much in high school." He will squirm and deny that he ever put it quite that way. If he merely squirms, like as not he was one of the boys who listened to other boys talking like that on the high school football field and laughed. If he squirms and turns red, he is lying.

Homophobes are quick to vilify love between women because the idea of women loving each other is diametrically opposed to volunteering yourself up for rape. The danger of women who love women, in the decrepit minds of patriarchal males, is that men may be challenged to love women too. No more "getting your rocks off." No more venting your frustrations on your wife. If you've got a problem, you'll have to solve it.

What else is there? Some man will have to answer that question. I am not about to help you to be more human; I have enough trouble doing that for myself. It is hard enough to reach inside myself and find my own humanity without carrying your load too.

I didn't always feel that way, as my friend Cj commented:

The Servant

> Lee, you make me hysterical
>   yes, you do
>   this white man wants to be served
> and you trot out your daisy apron
> and serve him
> in his own language!

Listen to the tone of the women who curse "Damn dyke!" It is filled with resentment and laced with a very mysterious kind of awe. You just know that "Who does she think she is?" follows closely on the heels of that first epithet. If we accept brutal sex as the best we can get, the norm, then naturally we are going to hate women who love women and don't have to put up with the violence that degrades most women in North America. Hate is itself perverse and so of course we get even by referring to dykes and faggots as diseased or mind-sick individuals.

Even the feminist movement has a hard time with love. I have heard it said that lesbianism is "women identifying with women." I admit I am at a loss for words that would embrace the very intimate love between two people who happen to be women. I am at a loss as to how to describe it as anything other than love between Sue and Carol, or whoever they happen to be. But calling it "women identifying with women" feels like a misnomer. Sex, love, intimacy are not about identification, they are bigger, deeper and broader than that. I am at a greater loss to describe the phenomenon here in North America where lesbianism has become a liberating force, as though it were an alternative to love. Having the freedom to love, be loved, determine the nature of the physical expression of that love, the power to name it, govern it, is liberating, whether the person you enjoy this freedom with is the same sex as you or different from you. It is just as powerful to enjoy the freedom to love with a man as it is with a woman. What is lacking for all women is the absolute right to be cherished and the absolute freedom to govern our love's expression.

All of our conversations about women who have women lovers are couched in terminology which escapes my comprehension: homosexuality, heterosexuality, lesbianism, homophobia . . . I have a very simple and straightforward philosophy, learned from my grandmother: "In the end, granddaughter, our body is the only house we will ever truly own. It is the one thing we truly own . . . What is more, in the end, command of it will only amount to the sacred right of choice."

From my grandmother's words I understand that there is human sexuality, a biological need for sex, and there is love. (All those who are easily embarrassed can put the book down.) Sex is sex. Sex and love are not the same thing and they are not equal. Sex is the one thing that we can enjoy completely on our own. (I suspect that a good many women do just that.) Few other animals have the wherewithal to gratify themselves sexually quite like we do. We do not need a partner or lover to have sex. When you up-grade sex to the level of love, you erase love completely.

When someone says she is a lesbian she is saying that her sexual preference is toward women. She is not saying that she does not like or love men. I have heard from women that so-and-so was bitter about her marriage so she went gay. It sounds so dangerously logical and absurd at the same time. It's as though "gay" were some place women go as opposed to, say, "shopping," and that there are only two attitudes women can have toward men, bitter and not bitter. Those who are bitter go gay and those who are not go shopping. The danger of the logic is that rather than respecting women as beings, it consigns them to going toward men or away from the men. It accepts that men and our attitudes toward them determine our sexual being. We get all tangled up in the web of our own misunderstanding and then ascribe that colossal ignorance to someone else.

Sex can sometimes go hand-in-hand with love. If it does, so

much the better. But it is not necessary to be in love to enjoy sex. When I first said that in public, an indignant, uncoupled woman said, "Well, sex and love have to go together." I responded brutally: "Yes, I am going to fuck my mother, my father, my sister, my daughters and all my friends." She didn't mean that.

What she thought is that women cannot have sex without love. Nonsense. I once went to a bar, looked around the room, saw a nice smile with a reasonable male body attached to it, walked over to the table and sat down. After a beer I grabbed hold of the gentleman's arm and let him know that any more of that stuff might impair his performance. To which he responded, "Are you interested in my performance?" I had hold of his hand already so I just nodded. "Why are we still here then?"

We left. The sex was not bad. There was no love, no illusions whatsoever, just the two of us rutting and being gratified.

Sex is good but love is precious. It is our passion and com-passion. Love defines our humanity. Focussed, love binds two people together in a relationship that can be lifelong. If we truly loved ourselves as women, the question of who we choose to engage with sexually would be irrelevant. Let us stop elevating rutting to the position of defining our humanity. Despite the pressure of sexually oriented billboards and TV ads, let us stop placing fucking on a plane alongside moral principles which confine women to being sexual vehicles rather than sexual beings.

The result of telling young women that they cannot have sex until they are married and in love is that the shame of desiring sexual gratification will mis-define their lives from pubescence onward. My daughters know, as all girls do, that if they want sex no one can stop them from getting it. It is one of the most avail-able commodities on the market, if you don't mind my cyni-cism. It is mis-defining their lives around sex that is degrading, and it usually comes from mothers at the behest of fathers.

Some mothers, in the interest of equality, try to convince their sons that they should also abstain from sex until marriage.

Pardon my heresy. I taught my children not to confuse love with sex, just as my mother taught me. I wanted them to learn about love from birth on. Surely we do not expect our babies to begin enjoying sex at birth. Is it love then that we seek to deny them? I am convinced that equating sex with love is what is behind all the perversity of child sexual abuse. Some people have taken the bullshit seriously.

The last little note I want to make on sex and sons is a curious one. We are dichotomous in the rearing of our sons and daughters. In order that our sons not grow up to be faggots, we teach them to be macho and to hate girls, loathe all that is gentle, loving and tender. We teach them to pursue sex with girls, who have been taught that sex without love is evil and immoral. We are ashamed when our daughters are discovered to be sexually active, but proud of our sons' sexual proclivity. "He is a real lady-killer." Listen to that: a killer, and we say it with pride.

Love is both a social and personal phenomenon. The dictates of individualism in North America put social love somewhere in the ashcans of the mind. I love men, but I choose one lifelong partner. I love women but sexually I prefer men, so the women I love will be enjoyed at the spiritual level and not the physical. Or the converse, I love men but prefer women sexually, therefore it is men who will be enjoyed on the spiritual level. Sound simple?

Love presumes the right to choose. That means it is no one's business but my own what goes on in my bedroom. Neither my children, my friends, my neighbours nor the world at large has the right to choose my partner. In fact, we don't practise that: our friends and families are notorious for pressuring us into choosing a "suitable" mate. Women influence their children to choose a partner that is compatible with them as mothers. Men extort from their sons the right to direct their choice of a lifelong partner. And yet we make loud noises about our freedom of choice compared to people in places like Africa and India, where arranged marriage is still a reality. In practice, there is little choice in partner selection, right here.

The right to choice is as false in this society as the right to be free. Feminists are fond of analyzing the practices of societies in Africa and pointing out the horrible roles of women in such places. Pointing fingers at the oppression of women elsewhere changes not a damn thing for women here.

Before we force women who love women to parade their intimate affection for all to examine, we should talk about rape—the kind that goes on in the home between partners. Before we ask women who love women to justify themselves, we had better talk about why we hate each other. And before we bestow the right on society to judge women who love women, we had better demand that society rectify itself.

The next time a woman asks me what my position on lesbianism is, I am going to ask her what her position is on her husband "getting his rocks off." If she gives me a straight answer, I am going to tell her that I am absolutely opposed to rape and that forcing anyone to accept my definition of who she may love amounts to rape.

To be raped is to be sexually violated. For society to force someone, through shame and ostracism, to comply with love and sex that it defines, is nothing but organized rape. That is what homophobia is all about. Organized rape.

4. My Love

A Lover's Reverie

Wind whisper softly in my lover's ear
caress his body with the words of our
ancestors

sun—riotous dawn—sun
awaken my eyes to the fine body
I have chosen to love.

I T HAS TAKEN so long to wade through the garbage heaped
upon us by a racist colonial society to find love. It has taken
us so long to really come together. I have brought pain and
terror into our bedroom. My lover has brought pain and anger.

A Lover's Lament

My darling—dare I call you darling
do the words of the foreigner

grate, painfully, against the flesh?

I am not the lover you think I am
Still, I want to be.
You need a sensitive lover
and I am only halfway there.

Somewhere along the road I must have taken on the settler woman's attitude, for I knew not how to love. Part of me craved your undivided attention, your absolute devotion. Part of me sought to free you and myself from this self-seeking madness.

I am torn apart and terrorized, not by you, my love, but by the war waging inside me. A new torment grips me for I know the battle will grow in intensity until my desire to love you without the need to use you prevails. As the war grows, so grows my madness.

I have no right to expect patience or ask you to carry on loving me in the face of madness. I do not ask you to forgive my behaviour nor do I expect you to forget. Secretly, passionately, I want you to help the patriot inside me win. Now you will be watchful, wary, waiting for my hysteria—the expression of internal war. Just as I am on guard against your anger, you watch for my hysteria. We are a pair of suspicious fools.

A love that cannot be trusted is a love that cannot be desired. You will tire of my hysteria, leave, and I will die a little inside. Not because of your departure, but at having been defeated one more time. For though I cannot love you as I want, still I want to.

A Lover's Desperation

Your eyes tell me you are weary
Your body tenses, you explode.
A sinking scream swallows me
it strangles my brain
my body trembles
I want to escape
Hide! Hide, quick!

more rage—the scream inside grows louder
my brain more senseless.

*Now, 'tis over. Blank. I am left with humiliation, indignity and the
awful nagging suspicion that this little scenario has put just a little more
distance between us.*

Fear requires courage to tame and subdue it. But courage
presumes self-confidence and I am insecure—battered. Like
promiscuity, insecurity is a faithless companion, for it only
begets greater insecurity.

Ghosts

Let's drink to the ghosts
    in our closet
not one beer for unity
love,
or the right to be free.

Here's a beer for the ghost
    of jealousy
that plague of pain
that surly beast of doubt.

Here, down a beer for the ghost
    of insecurity
the ghost that interferes
whenever paths cross.
another round for the ghost
    of rage
the one that boils over
each time a conflict we engage.
Let's drink especially to the ghost
    of terror

rage can't hold a candle to fear,
drink up then, drink to fear.

Drag them out of the closet
march them up and down
        before our eyes
drink to them, lest we forget
and bury them
        in our dim and distant past.

Let's not discuss a single thing
let us not be rational
that presumes we're human,
        warm,
        sensitive beings,
in need of patience,
        gentleness,
        and love.

The object is not unity
but to win this fight,
retaliate. Kick your lover's pride
dismantle his dignity
and drink,
        drink,
        drink . . .
to the ghosts
        in your closet.

If we ever stop celebrating
the ghosts in our closet

we will be forced to face
the enemy
and really fight.

TOGETHER

Those of you who think we ought to spend time choosing partners for other women will never experience love for yourselves. We have a great deal of work to do, undoing the hate we have for each other. We don't have time to choose partners for someone else. We, as heterosexually oriented women, may have difficulty accepting that other women have no sexual desire for men. Following this realization should come the realization that the journey of exploring our attitudes will broaden our humanity. By rejecting lesbians we close the door to our own journey.

5. Law, Politics and Tradition

I HID FOR A LONG time from the teachings of our ancient ones. Wary of the various self-proclaimed "spiritual leaders" who have occasionally danced across the pages of our recent history, I bent in the direction of European ideology. I must have felt that these self-proclaimed leaders misinterpreted the teachings of my ancestors. When my sickened spirit needed to be healed, though, I sought the teachings of my grandmothers. Not as a matter of course, but as a last straw. I found that many of our spiritual leaders were charlatans—caricatures of our past. But I also found that our sense of spirituality was very much alive and very much different from the urban "traditional movement" of the 1960s and '70s. (I thank Jeannette Armstrong, author of *Slash*, and her family for helping me make this discovery.)

The traditional movement was largely urban. Some of the people in the communities had never left themselves behind and, hence, had no need to find themselves or go back to themselves. I noticed that much of the traditionalism in the urban areas was coming from a very narrow few. These few had been highly mis-educated in the settler institutions and were full, inside and out, of settler traditions and ways.

Culture is the great separator that decides which direction a person will go when faced with a fork in the road. As a people, we have come to the fork many times. Some of us went one way and others went in a different direction. Those who held fast to the essential principles of their culture went in the direction of sovereignty; those who became alienated from their communities trod in the direction of sub-normal integration. There is a split within the elite—not an obvious split, but a split nonetheless. It reflects the two roads at the juncture of the '60s and the different direction that some of us took.

Let me state categorically: there are no enemies in the ranks of Native people. There are a number of people who seek power over others, but none of us has the slightest semblance of power. Someone who seeks power over others but lacks it in his daily life has the potential to become an enemy, should he realize his dream. He also has the potential to be a great and glorious leader should he realize the fallacy of his dream and alter his own goals.

There are those who choose a path of self-determination and those who choose a path of continued dependence. When our own people are faced with making a decision between one leader and another, they walk away. Beginning with residential schools, where powerless children ran away rather than rebel against the priesthood, most of us have learned to resist passively. Everybody run away! Still others accepted the endless moral arguments of the clergy and joined the fracas on the side of the priests. So it is today. There are those who oppose the corporate system of exploitation and those who would line up with it, against the rest of us.

Many of our people have adopted the ways of the settler. Distortion and deception are now an integral component of the culture of some of us. It happens that the Native elite, the miseducated middle class of our community, is loaded down with such people. This elite was created by Canadian government

funding and Canadian government-funded opportunities in the
sphere of education. This elite owes both its existence and its
loyalty to the piper that paid it to play the tune.

Some of the proponents of traditionalism advocate the internal apprehension of our children. Of course the funds to carry
out both the apprehension and the fostering out of these children will come from the government and go through this leadership.

If the elite would bother to look up the word "apprehension"
in the dictionary, they would realize that it means "terror."
Where in our traditions, laws or values was the terrorizing of
children acceptable? The other meaning of apprehension is tantamount to kidnapping. Where in our traditions, laws or values
was the kidnapping of a woman's children ever acceptable?

This is not the way to reduce unemployment in our villages.
If new parents refuse to look after their children, then the families of those parents will have to deal with that. There is plenty
of social work to be done around teaching youth our concepts
of child-rearing and adult responsibility to family. But it is
totally false to advocate the apprehension of children as a means
to resolve the problems of child-rearing and neglect, and to call
that self-government. To disguise settler culture and law with
the clothing of our ancestors is to mock the old laws.

Certain of the elite stood on our heads to climb out of the
mine shaft. They rely on our continued oppression to secure the
finer things of European life that they have come to enjoy.
Without our poverty they cannot justify their demand that
Canada grant them more crumbs. In the end, the only people
served by the attitude of some of the elite are the very people in
whose interest it is that we remain colonized.

To the elite, liberation means that they become our bosses.
Anything else amounts to so much treason, as far as many of
them are concerned. Just try and get up at any convention and
object to the direction in which they are leading us and you will
find yourself scorned. You will become the object of a system-

atic persecution such as we have not known since the United States cavalry chased Chief Joseph.

They will use any disguise to achieve their ends. Traditionalism has become the newest coat to cloak their hidden agenda. Most of us see through them. We know that you cannot have tradition without law. You cannot be lawless and claim reverence for the traditions of our ancestors.

Over and over again I have heard it said, "We were not a political people, we were a spiritual people." Let us acknowledge that the people saying this learned it in the same place I did —college. This philosophy was first articulated by an Englishman in the eighteenth century. It arises from a debate between European intellectuals over how to interpret our society as opposed to their society. In the debates between proponents of civil law and natural law, the adherents to natural law read very much like our modern-day urban traditionalists.

To accept a European interpretation of our old ways is foolhardy. Politics arises from law. To be without politics is to be lawless. To say our politics are in opposition to European politics would be correct. European law legalizes our oppression. Our law forbids it. But to say that we were lawless is to say that, indeed, we were savages.

I expect that Europeans cannot define our societies with any accuracy or draw connections between our society and their own. Further, I hardly expect them to be able to look at our laws and see the traditions, values and body politic that arise out of our legal system. I expect them to interpret history so as to justify their genocide against us in the name of humanity and civilization. But I did not expect our own people to parrot the racist formulators of sociology and cultural anthropology and call it "spirituality."

It is hard to watch the looks on the faces of our elders who are hearing this English terminology for the first time. Many of them lack the language skills of the youth and therefore accept that, in English, this is how our old ways are expressed.

However, they are not wholly sold on this bill of goods, as many of them revert to their own language and privately pray nothing gets lost in the translation. Few of us younger people know our old language. The language gap between generations is not going to be an easy one to close.

On the other side of the split are those people, young and old, from the Okanagan, the Gitksan-Wet'suwet'en, Iroquoian, Ojibway and Cree nations, who base their politics in their own history and their own law. There are intellectuals among them who did not lose themselves in the settlers' universities. Such intellectuals are precious gems in a sea of mis-education. They are a tremendous source of inspiration and empowerment.

In spite of the settler society and a long period of incarceration in settler schools, I have come to desire independence in my homeland. I say incarceration because the settlers' education achieved, for a time, its goal: the imprisonment of the Native mind in the ideology of the oppressor. Before I can understand what independence is, I must break the chains that imprison me in the present, impede my understanding of the past, and blind me to the future.

Without a firm understanding of what our history was before the settlers came to this land, I cannot understand how we are to regain our birthright as caretakers of this land and continue our history into the future. This understanding cannot come from the children of my generation alone. It must come from our elders' generation and the memories they cherish of their own grandmothers' words. The translators of the knowledge of our grandmothers must be well versed in their own language and in the language of the English people. And they must possess a deep sense of loyalty to our people.

I can only articulate my understanding of the laws that have survived and been bequeathed to me. I understand that the laws were obeyed not through armed force that was alienated from the people—such as police, army, etc.—but rather because the people agreed with the laws. In fact, they formulated them in the best interests of the community.

Therefore I can understand democracy. The will of the people was sacred to our leaders. This is one of our strongest traditions. No Native person accepts his or her leader's direction as a command. Conversely, only fools accept that a society that requires force to ensure proper social conduct is a democratic one. Without the voice of the trammelled and the dispossessed, democracy is but an echo in the canyons of the minds of lunatics.

I understand that my foremothers were an austere, disciplined people and were absolutely opposed to waste of any sort. Their standards of honesty were established by those people who contributed most to the well-being of the community and the nation as a whole. It was criminal to use another to enrich oneself; by this, I understand that exploitation of the land or people, in the interest of profit, was prohibited.

I understand that the teachings of my people were directed at instilling in our young children a sense of the self and our importance to the community. The teachings required that we seek not our own happiness but the well-being of others. This means that the self-indulgent ideology of "me first" runs contrary to our laws. In fact, individualism destroys the potential of each of us to contribute to the development of the nation. Worse, it narrows the development of the individual to a perverse form of consumerism. Thus, the luxury-oriented consumerism of this society runs contrary to our laws.

I understand that my foremothers were very conscious of their relationship with and dependence on the land as a source of life. They believed that to destroy life without necessity was a crime. More than that, to destroy natural life needlessly was to court disaster. This means to me that the destruction of natural resources and the production of junk, in the interest of profit, is contrary to our laws.

Further, if we are the caretakers of this land, then the obligation to alter the destiny of this society is our collective responsibility. The damage done to our homeland is our collective burden. To neglect the great cities of the nation as "bad places to
live" is just so much irresponsible negation of our obligation to
our history.

Here my understanding stops short. It is not possible for the
children of my generation to grasp our laws in all their complexity. We were raised in settler society, divorced from our past
and alienated from our history. Until all generations of our people come together to resume our birthright as caretakers of this
land, the future will remain unclear and the laws of the land will
not be known to us. I believe our elders will step forward and
educate us as soon as they see that we, young and not-so-young
adults, are seriously trying to take up our obligation to our
homeland.

6. Rusty

I MEANT THIS *to be a tender love story that came true. A fantasy of two people battering down the walls that separated them and erecting an arc—a bridge—to unite them. Instead the walls became reinforced with steel.*

I am but frail human flesh and can fight no more. I am battered and beaten, not by you, my love, but through pounding on the steel walls you hide behind. Where thin transparent glass was, thick steel now lives. You alone can dismantle the structure.

There was a basic flaw in your construction. You left little holes for me to peer through so that I might, with a great deal of effort, discern some of your hidden self. Was it through fear of being invisible and unloved or was it for love of me that you left the holes?

I don't know because I can't see.

When we each lived in a glass house we could both see. It required a mere shattering of the glass. I thought that night when you smashed my face that I had succeeded in breaking the glass house. When glass breaks someone gets cut. I did not mind being the one because I thought I had swung the hammer that broke the glass. But you built another wall.

I dare not tamper with steel.

It was sunny on the day they laid Rusty away. Death had not jarred my sensibilities since my grandma had died. Now youth in all its perfection lay in front of me, stilled by over-zealous living or a great desire to get life over with and die—I knew not which. She was in a not-bad-looking box, but nothing at all like the carved grave boxes of her grandmothers. I have been to a number of funerals since Rusty's and I still cannot get over the fact that dead, a person looks smaller. The spirit must occupy space.

Rusty, I didn't ever want to know your story, but since you gave it to me, I am going to give it back to the people responsible for it.

Rusty was not a "bush Indian." Her leanness stands out sharply. Her burnt brown hair against amber skin revealed her half-European heritage. She was raised in Vancouver, British Columbia, on Alexander Street, in an old house tucked in between the fish canneries and warehouses on the seedier side of the city. Not much changes on east Alexander Street. The old house is still there, its beige paint peeling and roof sagging just a little with age. It sits there, an anachronism from the past, mute testimony to another era in our history.

We had a little too much wine on this one night and Rusty started to talk about the kind of things we don't really want to remember or even know about.

The room I slept in was absolutely dark. The windows were broken and covered with cardboard and plastic. We never had lightbulbs for the overhead sockets. The wires were bare and the sockets needed an electrician to make them useable. I shared my room with my kid sister. It was about the size of a jail cell. I know, Christ, I have been in enough of them. It was crowded, but there is something terribly comforting about knowing that should something go awry, there is someone else there to share your fate.

In one corner was an old, unused water heater. The

bed took up more than half the room, wall-to-wall on one side. At the opposite end from the water heater, near the door, was a little dresser which hid our meagre wardrobe. There were other kids, but sister and I were close, and this story doesn't much concern the rest.

All week long, my dad would discipline us. On the weekend, with the help of some hard stuff, it would be my mom's turn. From the darkness I could hear them arguing. Soon the voices would drop and the sound of fists connecting with bodies would wind up the discussion. My sister was asleep but even so she did not escape the atmosphere. She would moan softly in her sleep, discomfited but too weary and accustomed to the violence that occasionally rocked our home to completely wake up.

In the dark, I would wander off. Eyes open, unseeing, I would think about the sounds of the fight, trying to know who was getting hit where and how. I used to feel bad about having made a game of my mother's pain. Now I know that children have to play. They make games of whatever life presents them with. If life gives them agony to play with, the games of children will be cruel jokes on the people that chart their lives.

Mama was deadly in a fight. A rodent. She would just sit and take whatever he dished out until she knew a well-placed blow would end it. Once it was boiling water. Another time, it was an iron skillet. Worrying about her survival stopped concerning me as much as it did when I was really small. I listened to the sounds and tried to predict the exact moment when she would strike.

One night, I realized that the fight was taking longer to stop than usually. Then, it got almost quiet. The old fear rose again. Involuntarily, my mind raised the possibility: What if she can't stop him? I got cold and my face was wet with sweat. The image of her small, lithe body, slowed and dogged by age, opposing his brute force, frightened me.

I tried to scream. My voice was locked up someplace far away from my body. Someone stole my mobility. My arms and legs were paralyzed. I was still alive, but my body didn't want to be, so it just left me unable to move.

Deep inside there was a war going on. I could feel it. The tanks and heavy artillery of my fear against my love for her, flying at each other. A militia of self-interest confused everything. I thought I would burst.

The war ended with my getting up. Too late. By the time I peeked around the corner into the kitchen, she was on the floor backside up. He was kneeling, holding her lifeless hips and moving back and forth. I didn't have a word for what he was doing, but I knew it was sick. I wanted to throw up. A little rubber mallet sat guiltily on the floor next to the scene of the crime.

I think I fainted because in the morning I woke up from a crumpled heap on the floor, my face still looking in the direction of the rubber hammer. No one was awake. She wasn't there anymore. Nor was he. I went back to bed. It is so hard to tell this part but, you know, I did not go to sleep in the natural way . . . It was more like slipping away . . . slipping away from life.

I crawled out of bed with everyone else. Mom seemed quiet and a little more humble than usual, her cheek-and-brass subdued, but otherwise everything seemed normal. Normal, but not natural. He was gone. I started doubting what I had seen. I argued with myself for a long time about whether or not I really had seen it at all.

Round about the time I had convinced myself that it had all been just a bad dream, Mom and I were walking downtown in the direction of the Army & Navy

department store. It was fall. No autumn leaves drifted
in the breeze on Alexander Street to let you know that
it was fall. It was the smell of the fish coming from the
canneries that determined the season: sockeye for this
time of year.

Out of the blue, Mom spat out the words, "I am
pregnant." Her voice was filled with secret fury. Tears
which I was sure were hot and red ran down her face,
but her voice remained steady. By now I had a word for
what he had done to her. "Christ, forty-two years old,
five kids and pregnant," she muttered. It sounded like
she thought she was committing a crime for having
gotten that way, even though I knew it was not her
fault. She had thought about an abortion, but finding
the money and the right quack who would do it without hurting her closed the door on that route.

I looked at the canneries and the fishing supply store:
the signs, whose paint was peeling and torn in places,
the bricks, black and red, all dirty from years of unpam-
pered living. I looked anywhere but at her. The nausea
of that awful night came back, but I felt no compassion
for her. The fucker had raped her, left all of us, and now
we were going to have to love his offspring. I stared at
the woman who found work so easy and mothering
children so hard, and I wondered how she was going to
be able to look after this baby. The white roots of her
hair beneath the black dye were showing again. I mentioned that her hair needed another dye job. Christ, talk
about a brutal kid.

She receded. Disappeared into the private world of
the uncared-for. If I had really heard what she was saying and responded, she would have told me the rest.
She would have felt better. Her spirit would not have
flagged. Now silence separated us. It was the last time
she offered herself to me.

Maybe so, Rusty, but you are using a woman's insight to judge a child, which is just a little unfair. If you had responded as a woman, then, you would not have needed a mother. We are going to have to stop expecting so little from our parents and so much from our children. Everything seems to be upside down right now.

In the darkness of my room I cried out for forgiveness and begged her to love me. It was too late. Her spirit just up and left—jumped into the ever-present wine bottles that men and her good looks brought. Funny, men are so quick to bring in the booze and so slow to buy you a meal. I remember crying in the night, night after night; then, nothing.

She died before I ever found the balls to tell her I was sorry. I wish that had been the end of it. After she died the dirty dog came back. He came to fix me up for the rest of my days.

Well, the wine bottle was showing signs of depletion, being drained as it were, by the two of us. I was beginning to feel like I wanted to be somewhere else. I was wishing I could get up and leave the room without hurting Rusty, but I couldn't, so I stayed. That struggle to find a reason to leave without dragging along the guilt of deserting someone was the beginning of an age-long battle in me. I still do it. I never want to stay, but someone roots me to the spot until whoever is speaking to me has passed on their misery. *I knew that you were going to tell me all about it, Rusty, that you weren't going to spare me.*

He must have seen me there, a bunched little brown heap on the floor. When he grabbed me and hissed that I was not his kid and that that meant he could do what he liked with me, I had the feeling that his kid or not, that was a lie. I was terrified about the meaning of "what he liked," but relieved that I would never again have to shame myself with his paternity. He mentioned that I deserved more than my mama got. Then, he laughed. At twelve, I didn't fight back. Lee, I didn't fight back. I can still hear him laughing right this minute.

We were alone. I sank into a kind of odd oblivion when he grabbed me. I prayed to all my grannies that somewhere out there, please let there be a man I could love. Of all the things to think about. Pathetic.

All I saw was that pink thing coming down at my face in the middle of a mass of white skin. I heard him warn me not to bite. When it was over, he was laughing and I was vomiting. I swore to my grandmothers before me and my grandchildren after me that no white man would ever have my love. I swore to make myself the finest Native woman possible and withhold my affection from the people that reduced me to the sub-human.

All I remember is that pink thing coming down toward my mouth, the sick, puking feeling rising in my stomach and the laughter. I hated white men after that. For a long time the sight of a shirtless white man made me want to throw up. They'd get theirs. I vowed to avenge my womanhood, my youth. When I was through, a trail of broken white boys would be strewn behind me, bewildered by the extraction of their affection and the bareness of my heart. In high school I watched the boys and found out that what they wanted from Native girls was not the same as what they wanted from their own.

What white boys wanted in dark meat was not the coy, flirtatious routine of white girls but the subtle mysticism they thought dark-skinned girls had a monopoly on. They wanted sultry silence and intense submission, a wise façade without their own women's smugness.

They wanted the self-effacing surrender of a dark
woman to white superiority. They wanted a ready
Mona Lisa half-smile and a gregarious enjoyment of
their need to be the centre of a dark woman's attention.
They were thrown into a frenzy by dark-skinned sensuality . . . If it was withheld they would go mad.

I learned to fight, Lee. When you don't surrender,
they try to force their attention on you. It is not quite
the same as the rape I had experienced at my "Dad's"
hands. It was more like aggressive sex, rough seduction.
More than one white boy was shocked and humiliated
by the thought that he had almost raped me. There is
one curious side to white boys that I had not known
before. Did you know that they whine and beg while
they are tearing at your clothes? I think that if I had
ever married one of them, he would not have outgrown the shame. You know what I mean?

I thought at the time that I did know what you were saying, Rusty,
but now, in the starkness of a grey and windy autumn morning, dead
leaves fluttering about in near silence, I am not sure if you meant they
would not have outgrown the shame of having come close to rape or the
shame of having begged for your affection. At the time I was reading the
answer from your face. Now, the face is dim and only the words are clear.

Tearing at my clothes and wrestling with my resistance,
breathing hard, almost frantically, the white boy would
suddenly jump to his feet. The realization that he was
using force hit him in the face. Then he whimpered
that he was not an animal . . . that I was a tease . . . that
I drove him out of his mind with desire, and other such
stupidities. Each one was the same as the one before
and the ones that came later. It was like a re-run with
the same actors playing the same parts over and over
again.

It was sick. I was sick. I intended to saturate myself with their pain and expunge my own. It didn't work. I do not know if I ever really thought it would. By the time I was seventeen, the only thing I was soaked with was an overwhelming desire to stop the show.

After a six-month downward spiral into the world of alcohol and the street, I decided to have another go at life. One slow afternoon in front of the telly, I watched that woman. You know, the Black woman whose husband was a preacher, a civil rights leader in the States. Coretta King. She was drivelling a lot of nonsense. Then, quite by accident, I was sure, she said something profound: "We are going to bring love and dignity back to our people." Love your own, she said. I had been so busy hating white men that I had almost killed myself. It was all so ridiculously simple—just love your own.

Something tragic must have happened to all of us somewhere along the line. Jeezus, Lee, I think we hate ourselves. Around every corner, you can find some nice white do-gooder all hyped up to love Indians, but it is real hard to find one of us to love us. There is no "white trash" kickin' at us anymore—we are doing it to ourselves.

I am beginning to feel like our own men do not want us. They don't like us. We are just here for them to vent their frustrations, just whipping posts, if you know what I mean. Worse, we are with them because they couldn't get a white woman.

We were getting down to the wire. I finally figured out that all this was just background material for what Rusty really wanted to say. Her lover was an Indian, a Native who was anything but a gentle man. "How did you meet him, Rusty?" Gawd, I must have been seven kinds of fool to invite her to tell this story. I knew I was not going to be able to forget it.

Pigeon Square, park bench #3. He was just lying there. Newspapers lined the bench and covered his face. It was kind of comical when he woke up. He had been lying face down with his head turned to one side. There were some letters imprinted on his face, bass-ackward. You wouldn't believe what they were—"Indians" spelled backward on his cheek. He was pretty as a picture, even unclean and still half-crocked. Jeez, I wish I had never met him. He is making it so hard.

There is a storm of passion locked up in every person's being, a storm that is intense but not disquieting. A tornado without a vortex. A wind that is erratic, directionless and incessant. At the same time, there is no wind at all. Just a flood of passion without beginning or end. A passion quietened only by sensuous satisfaction. Passion that is satiated by physical expression and is only free to rise again, invigorated by its own realization.

Our first night was like nothing I have ever known. Over and over again the flames of passion were rekindled by its satisfaction. The morning came too soon. Dawn is always brutal in its presentation of reality. We did not know each other, had never seen each other before yesterday. I hated to even look in the mirror.

Shower, groom and dress; then breakfast and off to work. The reality of what had occurred was a cold blast of air on a warm spring day. I felt imprisoned by the speed of my submission—submission without any commitment. I was locked into the realization that I did not know this man, merely desired him. Shame floated about in the atmosphere I travelled in. I was not his friend, had just barely made his acquaintance. He offered nothing and owed me less. It was as though the revelry of the night before was all that I had coming to me.

Silence prevailed. Silence became the structure of the prison we were erecting for ourselves. I sat eating the eggs he had cooked and wondered who was inside and who was outside the prison walls. I was to learn much too late that it was I who was locked outside his cell. The prison of his being was self-imposed and he enjoyed it.

The storm that is passion is wonderful, exhilarating, but unrequited love is steady torment. I arrived at work on time each day, ritualistically buried the fallen, educated those who would work. I learned to laugh above the sound of my mind listening for him. I typed while my eyes watched for him. I stared long and hard at his name written in the guest book each second or third day. I never once lied to myself, though. He avoided me and came in with other company when I was not there. It didn't matter. Seeing his name in the guest book conjured up a pleasant film of that single night that I alone possessed. Lee, I stupidly let him into my life after that.

Stupidly? Not stupidly, Rusty. The absence of dignity in our lives precludes self-respect. We have given up respect and therefore we can't love.

You know, Lee, an old person once told me to stop turning over stones and looking for crabs or I would get pinched. I never really figured out what that meant until after I lived with this man. You know the scenario. The first time he beat me up it was because I seriously shamed him. After that, the crimes got smaller until he just whacked me as a matter of course. He was turning over stones looking for crabs all the time.

Funny thing. After you tell yourself that first time that you had it coming, there is always this little suspicion that you had this one coming too, even when

there is no objective reason to feel that way. You start to
think that you could have done this or that to avoid a
beating. Even if you didn't deserve it, you somehow
think that if you could have avoided it and didn't, in
some twisted way it was your own fault.

Anyway, ol' girl, the story is getting to be a drag. I
better quit before the big bad wolf gets home and hears
me talking like this.

Her wolf wasn't going to return. We both knew that. He had
taken to keeping company elsewhere for weeks at a time. Since
he had just left that day, he wasn't due back for a good while. I
didn't tell Rusty that I knew he had not been sharing the cost of
living with her since he had started straying. I am glad that I did
not add further embarrassment to her dilemma.

*What you really meant, Rusty, was that if you kept talking like that
you would have to do something about it. You couldn't, none of us
could. You tried to sort it all out, to find a way to look at it all without
dying inside.*

A light cloud obscured the sun. A tiny mist of darkness covered
the funeral scene. Rusty is lying there, all the fight knocked out
of her, and rape is on my mind. I, too, have had to fight over
and over for my womanhood. After thirteen short years, I
learned that the world hates women and "squaws" do not even
qualify as women.

My mind drifts back to the kitchen of my home long ago,
where my mother sat rolling a cigarette and telling a story. I was
sick and had been for a long time. My younger brother was gur-
gling and sitting up in his tenda. I had lost a piece of his life. At
birth his hair was light gold, his eyes were blue. Now they were
big and brown. I vaguely remembered his homecoming, the
fight over his name and the disappointment about the colour of
his eyes. Mama had started a regular job about then. I remembered her first day of work after the baby came home. We all

lined up to say good-bye. She was smiling, but there was a film of sadness behind the smile that never went away. We were all so proud of her. Mama had a job.

That is all I remember until that day in the kitchen, watching Mama roll a cigarette. My older brother was jumping on the bed and Mom told him not to. I can hear her voice telling him that I was going to be all right, but that I was still sick and couldn't play yet. I meant to ask how long I had been sick after Mom finished her story.

A young girl, not yet thirteen years old, had been raped and killed and left in the gravel pit not far from our home. Mama wanted us girls to know that there were some terrible men in this world. She wanted to spare us the agony of rape. Over the years, I watched my mama struggle hard against her revulsion for men who would violate women. I watched her venomous attacks turn to long discourses on rape and how to deal with it. She was preparing us for the inevitable.

She wanted us to loathe and detest rape and the men who would commit such acts, yet not be cynical about men in general. "Most men are not like that," I can still hear her say. "Men who rape women, hate women. They are a minority—a sizeable minority, but a minority nonetheless." Her beautiful face tilted upward toward the light as she purred softly, "Don't let anyone try and kid you, rape has nothing to do with lust. It is all about hate. Fight back. Resist. No woman has to accept violence in any form."

Mama, you were right about the hate, but wrong about its rarity. For us, rape is not an oddity but commonplace. I have had to fight over and over again for my life. My life. A woman does not get over rape any more than a man "gets over" castration. (I am not speaking of the kind of castration whining men are always accusing assertive women of committing because they cannot handle equality between the sexes, but the castration of Black men lynched by white men, where manhood is actually removed.)

Rusty didn't live long enough to get past the point of trying to look at her reality through the hazy glass of a wine bottle. Suicide has plagued me since we buried Rusty. Friend after friend cashed in their chips and died at their own hands. Guilt and the agonizing notion that I could have saved them has dogged me.

> Save them for what, Lee? For the pain they couldn't deal with? You know, Lee, that is the one thing they can't take from us. The one power we really have is to decide when we are going to exit.

I wish life had been easy for you, Rusty. There you are, lifeless in that box, your body sucked dry by the very person you tried hard to love—yourself. Neither of us knew then that loving ourselves was the very thing we would find hard for a long time.

We find it easy to be bodily passionate with each other—physically free and seemingly caring. But it is nearly impossible for Native men to cherish the femininity of Native women. They have grown up in a world in which there is no such thing as dark-skinned femininity. There is only dark-skinned sensuality.

For a woman to love a man, she must first love herself. Both must humble themselves to each other. What could be worse than two sub-humans reduced to humbling themselves to some half-beast that doesn't have feelings? We are a conquered people. Spiritually dead people, warmed up and forced to behave as though we were alive. I am certain it is because we have been raped. Our men know that we have been raped. They watched it happen. Some of the rape we have been subjected to was inflicted by them. Some of them were our fathers and our brothers. We are like a bunch of soft knots in dead trees, chopped down by white men, the refuse left for our own men-folk.

And Rusty's words echo in my ears.

Do my brothers think me blind? When I saw my man looking at magazines of naked white women in front of me and heard him laugh voluptuously while he leafed through the pages, the reality of my raped womanhood, my erased femininity came alive. Do you think me blind, brother, that I don't see you looking with approving eyes at other women—mostly white—while I am trying to reach out and talk to you? Do you think me blind? When we were out together, you stared at the beautiful, half-naked singer while I spoke softly, seductively, trying desperately not to be erased.

When you laughed about the white girl in your high school, twirling her baton while her suit split wide open, I couldn't help but think, Where does that leave me? When you laughed and told me what you had done to hurt one of the Native women you supposedly loved, did you see me wonder what you laughed about behind my back? When I heard you had laughed about your "hiding on me," I saw that pink thing coming down at me and asked my grandmothers to help me: "Put your timeless loving selves inside me. Help me to love myself enough to love my own."

I thought then that I would like to love you enough so you would love yourself. But I cannot do anything for you. You will have to find that on your own.

When you went drinking with that white woman you worked with instead of coming home to dark meat and a house full of children, did you see me in your mind? Or did you erase me? When you told my crazed spirit that it was not your habit to phone me and tell me where you were, as though I did not deserve your respect, I asked again for the strength to love.

One day, quite deliberately, I did not ask for help. I fought. The women in your life had all given up on you. They are women who know love is impossible. At best, we can achieve the lust of our men-folk if we dress right, emulate white women and mimic their seductive manner. Made-up and painted, such women have given up on our men-folk.

I cannot seduce or offend your manhood. It is not lust that I desire but to know your spirit. Lust and sensuality are nice but I can get that from any man. If we are only deserving of lust, then our men are reduced to the level of studs, bucks and fools.

I confess, I used to be that way. I did seduce men. It was not hard. Their spirits were all mangled and the women in their lives had already crushed what was left. Why we seek to conquer with lust the very people that could love is beyond me.

I want to heal your spirit and awaken the manliness that keeps trying to come alive in you. I can see it under the veneer you have covered it with. I can feel it in your rage and in your meanness at times. I can see it in the sadness on your face. The heartache written there was not put there by me or you. It is maintained by your succumbing to it.

Reflections from the Summit

I am not a rose in your lapel.
I am an annoying dandelion.
Useful to you
should you want to bring
          love to our community.

I am useless to a middle-class aspirant.
Harmful to someone who wants to live
above the poverty line,
enjoy luncheons on Friday
and dine out twice monthly.

I subtract
from your ability
to vacation once per annum.
I stand in the way of your need
     to be only half there.

I am an asset to a man
who seeks liberation
from the death colonialism is.
Valuable to a man
     who seeks escape
from the lonely castles
     built for the elite.

I am passion,
bright red and turbulent,
vehemently cutting a swath
through this brick, steel
     and concrete tundra.

I am compassion,
soft, warm and winsome,
pleadingly coaxing gentleness
from the burning anger
     of your spirit.

I am yours
in a way you don't understand.
I loved you
despite the cold wind
     of your storm
bequeathed to me by enemies.

I am yours
despite the shame
your wanderings brought.
Yours, despite the pain
of your great pummelling arms,
your deceitful lashing tongue.

I have taken of your flesh
what love you had to give.
I have tasted your sweet manhood,
touched your urgent passion,
brought you to desire
      and spent it.

I am yours.
I have seen your twisted spirit,
dried your eyes when betrayal
      caused you to weep.

I have seen you
in your finest moments
      in battle
against your scarred
      and wounded self.

I have seen you
      move mountains.
At the summit, I watched
      helplessly,
while you tried to bury me.

You wanted so much
      to climb alone.

You never wanted to face
that you needed the help
of a tearful woman.

I have withstood quite well the insult to my womanliness that
racism naturally gives rise to. It is common practice for white
and non-white boys to acquire their first taste of sex at our
expense. It is not required that anyone love us—we are by definition incapable of womanly love. It is aggressive sex that we
get—passionate body language but no spiritual affection.

I can handle that; being unloved is hard, but being raped is
death. It forces women to withdraw from the world of men, to
seek pleasure dispassionately. To withdraw from the world of
men and passion because of rape is to self-impose spiritual
blindness and offer ourselves up to the prison we create in the
darkness of our rooms.

In the darkness of my room, I am constricted by the terror of
a sightless life. Not just the physical blindness of not seeing
colours, smiles and grey concrete sidewalks, but the blindness of
not acknowledging the spiritual truth of a thing. It is frighten-
ing to act without appreciation—to move without seeing, only
feeling the locomotion of your body. Rape is like that.

The wind blew softly against my face and the pallbearers closed
the box and gently lowered it into the hole. I could hear the
grasses breathe a sigh of relief and feel the earth welcome
Rusty's return.

*I would have cried, Rusty, but for the fact that 'tis I who will be hear-
ing your story in the darkness of my room.*

7. *Black Robes*

THE CHILDREN OF our people must seek knowledge
wherever life presents it. Black Robe was a new thing;
thus, she was there in the green meadow where Mexica
horses lolled about, clipping grass and enjoying the soft warmth
of mother sun. Here, indeed, was something different. Word-
lessly, she absorbed its newness.

Black Robe seemed agitated. He spoke fast, and later the girl
learned from her father's account to her mother that he never
repeated his listeners' words as we do (very rude). She heard
everything Black Robe said only because her father spoke in the
old way. He was careful to repeat Black Robe's words verbatim,
to show respect for the speaker's vision of truth and to ensure
that no misunderstanding or distortion of his words occurred.
Then, her father answered him.

"There is only learning and knowledge, Black Robe. We do
not deny our children knowledge. You say that you have teachers who will show my children how to live. Can you not see?
Behind me sits my daughter, who is neither blind nor deaf nor
imprisoned. She is free to seek knowledge among whomever

she chooses to learn from. Her presence among adults indicates her desire to know. Hence, are we not obligated to give her our knowledge whenever she walks among us? You see her. She will have no need of interpreters if we continue to counsel, you and I. What need, then, has she of this place called 'school'?

"Her brothers and she can learn things that we cannot teach them, like medicine, sanitation, housekeeping and flight, you say." Her old father laughed. "When she grows wings and learns to fly, will she also acquire the beauty and sense of freedom of the eagle, the brazenness and wit of raven? Will her eyes see at night like owl? Black Robe, show me how you fly and my daughter will fly tomorrow; then, she will have no need of canoes. It takes a long time to build a bridal canoe.

"You say she will learn not flying, but different things than her brothers; that her brothers will learn about flying in something of their own making, not by themselves. In a glider, you say. That they will not actually make such a thing but only know of its existence. Of what use is such knowledge? You will fill my young men's minds with useless knowledge, Black Robe. You say my daughter will learn how to be a good Christian wife, to do a thing called read from deadwood leaves. What need has she to be a woman different than what she is? To kill trees and put marks on the deadwood leaves to remind her of how she must conduct herself? She is not lazy, nor is she forgetful. She is a good girl and will become a good woman. She will make a good wife—maybe Pierre's wife," he teased. She blushed and looked at the ground. Her old father chuckled sensuously.

Black Robe sucked in his breath. (I should not say this, nor even think it, but written on his face was exasperation, like when a young girl weaves her first basket and her fingers disobey the heart and will not weave it right.) The interpreter interjected, trying to bring depth to Black Robe's shallow vision of life. He tried to make the father and Black Robe see each other's point of view; to make them understand that there is no disagreement over the value of different (new) knowledge, but only a difference in how to learn—at home, or far away, with children from many different villages.

The interpreter is not speaker or listener, so neither Black Robe nor the father responded. But his words stayed with the young woman. She looked hard at the interpreter. She knew that her father would not relent. Her eyes tried to tell the interpreter that Black Robe was wasting his time. She wanted to save him more embarrassment. Soon the father would look upon his pleas as begging. No woman should sit and watch a man reduce himself to a beggar without first warning him. Black Robe was blind to the young woman's eyes and the interpreter dared not say what he thought he saw in the young woman's eyes.

Black Robe did not stop talking.

In the end, the father did not relent, but he invited Black Robe to counsel whomever he pleased. "Turn anyone around that you may, Black Robe." It was for her father a great and generous concession.

His prophecy about the young woman and the interpreter came to be. Pierre Deneuve, a man whose father came from a place called France and his mother from her own people, came to be her partner.

Partner. Husband in English. She learned to understand this immodest and mean language which has so many names for the same man; as though they were the land, not men from such-and-such a land. She never bothered to speak the language much, and, by the time I came to be it was hard for her to speak English.

In the warmth of her kitchen the soft tones of her voice touched my ears and gentled my raucous spirit. She brought me sadness but once in the multitude of after-school days I spent in her kitchen. I had learned not to query uselessly before I learned to speak. This day I mentioned all my great-grand-mothers and how I would like to see them. She could not give me their presence; instead she gave me her story.

"Pierre tried to teach me all the new things he knew, but

0008999360

Sell your books at
World of Books!
Go to sell.worldofbooks.com
and get an instant price
quote. We even pay the
shipping - see what your old
books are worth today!

they never made sense." She winced and laughed mischievously. "He said that he was a Christian, a Catholic, an interpreter, a Half-breed, a worker, and not just Pierre. To me, he was always Pierre. The funniest thing he said was that he was a Roman Catholic. Rome is in a place called Italy—far away. How could he be from here and from Italy?"

She stopped laughing. Silent, gentle tears flowed from her tired eyes. "He made me send my children to school. All my babies, I knew them only while they were small. They came home men and women. So different were they from me. So many of their words grated on my being, foreign words, like Pierre's. So little did they speak their own language. Today, I am surrounded by the faces of our people speaking as the Black Robes spoke. In the faces of the children are written the characters of the people of the Black Robes. The laughter of my ancients died in the house that Pierre built.

" 'My brothers, my sisters are all dead from the Black Robes' disease or killed in their wars. How can you ask me to send my little ones to grace their presence and not shorten my own life with their smiles and their growth? Will you call me wife, yet deny me motherhood?' I asked him."

She said that Pierre had said a lot of nice things to ease her pain, but he sent the children. "Of what use were nice words? Was he standing at the precipice of our son's grave—my son— alcohol-crazed, screaming insane words at a room with deaf walls, in a dirty hotel, while alcohol ate the life from his body? No. The Black Robes' disease had already taken his life and it was I who had to bury my son. All mothers ever ask of life is to die before their children. I have buried four of mine. Worse, now I must bury my tiny little grandchildren."

She whispered in the language of the old people, a language she forbade me to speak lest the craziness of her sons and daughters who had died overtake me. Lest I have no one language but become a crippled two-tongue.

"Master their language, daughter; hidden within it is the way

we are to live among them. It is clear that they will never go
away. Every year more of them come. England, France, Wales—
all must be terrible places, for they keep coming here to get away
from there. I do not begrudge them a place here, but why do
they have to bequeath to us the very things they escape from?"

It was like that in the 1950s in the wood-smoked kitchens of
our grannies. I thought then that I would join the lonely march
of six-year-old children going to grow up in the convent, missing my mom and unable to speak to my brothers. What a shock
when school arrived and I was thrown not among Native children, but Europeans. The teacher was not a nun, but an ordinary white woman.

Back in my granny's kitchen I was in tears, complaining
about not being with the other children. She watched me weep
until a deep sense of the foolishness overtook me and stopped
the flow of my tears. "You are fortunate. How else will we ever
master the language and keep our ways unless we can learn
among them and still live with our mothers and grandmothers?
You are fortunate. How else will we learn to master their ways
and still master the ancient art of motherhood unless we are
schooled by them and our mothers too? Further, it is not our
way to bring misery to others. Better to teach them to treat you
as a human being ought to be treated than to come here making
gifts of misery to an old woman who has done you no harm."
Her silence spelled dismissal.

At age ten I stood at the edge of my granny's grave, surrounded by Europeans, and witnessed the burial of our ancient
ways. I wondered if the birth of a new world founded on the
coming together of both our histories was really possible.
Would Europeans ever look at me and see an equal, not an
aborted cripple but a human being with all my frailties, my separate history, and our common future? I would not have had
such thoughts if the grandmothers of this land had not battered
themselves with the question, mused aloud in the presence of
their granddaughters.

Had mass death, tuberculosis, and the loss of our grandmothers' right to raise their young not have accompanied the development of Canada, the settlers would not have thought thus. Should we have been invited not as inferior sub-humans, but as people with a great contribution to make to the creation of a new nation, death would not haunt us as it does. More, our disappearance from the realm of history—the lingering realization that to most Canadians we do not exist—would not be our intimate agony.

Racism is an essential by-product of colonialism. That Europeans came here to escape something may be true, but it was not the real reason for erecting a colonial colossus all over the world. It was not the reason for the enslavement and importation of millions of African citizens to work our lands and build a meaner system than the world had ever known.

Europeans today see Natives without being able to imagine our grandmothers. They never see the old women who shaped our lives: the ankle-length flowered and paisley cotton skirts; the warm earth colours of their clothes; the kerchiefs and laughing eyes are lost to Europeans. They can never hear the soft tones of our grandmothers' ancient languages.

Europeans are blinded by Hollywood images. How sad. Not for me, but for them, as humanity is forever lost to those who would object to the colours and voices of the people of the past that have left their mark on the hearts and minds of the people of the present.

As a child I was humiliated by a string of teachers wearing brothel-tinted sunglasses. I was accused of sluttish behaviour by a moralizing principal whose assessment of me was guided by the colour of my skin rather than my character. Now that line of teachers looks pathetic and the poetry of T.S. Elliot burns new meaning onto the pages of my own book: "We are the hollow men / the stuffed men . . ."

I no longer weep for myself or the lost Europeans, but rather insist on writing myself into a new book that counts all of humanity on its tender, warm and colourful pages.

We are not an integrated people. We do not even co-exist peacefully. The reality of death still mangles our existence.

Black Widow-maker

Death hangs over us
like a black widow-maker
on a treeless mountainside.

A beleaguered army
caught in a valley
we thought green, lush
and teeming with life
   suddenly becomes a swamp
   full of alligators
   leeches, filth and disease

DIS-EASE

Caused more by the shame
of being fooled one more time.

In the darkness of our own
confusion we have forgotten
our reason for being.

In our grannies' kitchens, where the scent of wood smoke and sumptuous meals cooked over a thousand fires lingered in the unpainted walls and cupboards, that is where I learned the laws which enabled me to love my children. In my granny's kitchen, the sweet smells and gentle words soothed the aches and pains of a six-year-old growing up in a schizophrenic situation. Unlike in school, in my granny's kitchen I was not made to memorize or even contemplate the meaning of her words.

"You will remember what you need to know when the time comes." Right then, it was the sunshine of her presence that I needed. Her radiance was neither finite nor momentary. It is this shower that I bequeath to my children.

Her love was not without discipline, but it did preclude violence. I searched her story for some parable, and after many years realized there was none. She could not give me my ancestors. I would have to find them myself. Not to let me walk away empty-handed, she gave me herself. She must have known I was desperate, for she never shamed me for begging. I was desperate, so desperate.

Before the fires of maddened Blacks burned their anger onto the face of a frightened white America and made it forever impossible to erase African-Americans, there was sleep. The sleep of fools who know what they do but don't think of the consequences of their actions. It was the sleep of an insipid historical continuum that repeated its idiocy, not just by force of habit, but because no one raised any objections.

Force is the midwife of historical change.

"It was the best of times and the worst of times . . ." We need only add, "and the stupidest of times," and we will have painted the prosperous '50s in the bleak colours of mass insensitivity and righteous, red-neck practice. In the '50s there was no challenge. The Red "man" was vanquished—consigned to a kind of living purgatory in curio shops and tourist-trap trading posts. The Black "man" was reduced to a toe-tapping bundle of rhythm. (Black and Red women did not exist for anyone, yet.) All the Natives were happy, and working-class Europe-cum-CanAmerica was movin' on up.

Before Rusty and Alexander Street,
skid row and my children
there was my grandmother.
On the shore by the lakes
and in the hills of our heritage,

our grannies sat on deadwood logs
behind the Black Robes
and their fathers.

8. The 1950s

"IN CANADA, we are all middle class," the teacher said, parroting the spirit of neo-colonialism, and then dressed down the foolish lad who arrived at school coatless. Obviously, he had forgotten his coat. That he did not own one was a shock which would not shake the peace of CanAmerica until it was much too late for him.

"Have you forgotten your lunch again?" The shame of having to admit that he had no lunch to forget was too much for him to bear. In school, he learned that he did not measure up to his own people's standards. On the street, he learned he did not matter. In jail, he learned that solitary confinement was not the best way to withdraw from heroin. When he came out, he learned that the world had not changed, but instead, had become entrenched in its debasement of all that was not parasitic and respectable. He withdrew from the world—stretched at the end of a belt—this European boy who had no mother or history to save him.

No wood smoke or pungent odours of the old ways to remind him of what was, or could be. He perished. Still, when they wrote his story on their deadwood leaves for all the world to see, they referred to him as a young man, generously affording him his manhood and his youth. It is no comfort to his brothers and sister, but honestly, I am weary of reading about "Indian females" when they recount our deaths for all to see. Mostly they don't even count 'em.

Heartless teachers come to mind. Teachers who knew that Annie had died while we were kicking ball on the street in front of my house, but didn't care to hear the desperate screams of her sons as they ran after the ambulance which chugged her body away. It was a bizarre scene: white-skinned legs, reddened by the mid-summer sun, entangled with the leathery legs of the neighbourhood Half-breeds, all desperately trying to catch the car that denied us one last good-bye. Which teacher heard Annie's little boy cry?

"WA-AITT"

"WA-AIT, MOM!"

"I'm COMING!"

"WA-AIT FOR ME, MO-OM!"

Sweet Annie could not wait. Grandmother, why did she have to take the laughter and sparkle of her son's eyes with her? Did she need his loving glance to comfort her for all eternity?

Children didn't exist for these teachers. They taught students. They taught the acquiescent the rules of acceptance. They helped those who didn't fit to shave off pieces of themselves to make them fit, but they did this only for the willing. There were those among the student population who were unwilling.

For all the shame I withstood in the 1950s, for all the derision I endured for being what I was, I am still the same person today. The dictates of good taste prohibited the consumption of bannock and pickled herring, yet today, they are still my favourite foods. So I was outrageous?

"Why do you always stink?"

"It's just my nasty disposition." Another prospect of friendship died in the lap of cheek-and-brass resistance. It kept me alive. Were you all surprised when the children of America, the "darkies," stood up, rioted or got just plain rude with their rebellion? You shouldn't have been. We all learned it at your fine schools.

"Why do you wear those cheap and gaudy beads when you should know they make you look so Indian?" the teacher purred gently.

"I didn't think it showed."

Her back arched simultaneously with her brow. A few kids sniggered. Recovering herself she dripped, "How quaint, you want it to show, don't you?" It was too late. I had mastered the language of the Black Robes. The important words for me were not the ones you wanted me to learn. In Catholic school, you taught my cousins such words as "turn the other cheek," but in your own institutions you taught me "justice for all." I believed in these words. I wanted them to be true. I learned that others had fought for such things as human rights and justice and won. I learned that in the realm of justice, you did not count me. The words you saved for me were imprisoned words, locked in colonial bias. You tried to restrict my movement and teach me words that would help me to accept my own imprisonment.

> . . . and the rain of our green meadows
> mingled with tears of pain,
> pain healed by earth's soft damp.

From early spring until late fall, every sunny day found me in the meadow behind my home. I lay there and felt the embrace of the green grass. I tried hard not to let my anger consume me. I soaked up the earth's warmth and let the sting of racist attitudes pour onto my mother beneath me.

Before Birmingham, the burning of Watts and the Prince Rupert riots shook European North America naked of its silk gown of apathy, before Vietnam and the slaughter of Mexican students emboldened Native people in Canada to pick up the

broken thread of their lives, there were only green meadows and
rain to assure us that life was a constant and our social condition a
variable. Before all that, there were a host of teachers and the rain.

> Wounds. Scars.
> Cherished and held precious
> until the teachings of our grannies
> everywhere were resented.
> Scars that were stored up
> and buried with the entombed grannies
> of our homeland.

"Sometimes to straighten bamboo we must bend it in the
opposite direction," we were told. We bent. We bent until we
no longer heard the words of the elders. We no longer "spock
brocken inklish" but mimicked Shakespeare and Liza Doolittle
to a fault. The dollies of the integrated Native elite were born
with backs bent round with the effort. We doubled over until
we crawled. All Europe thought we were integrated. We knew
we were disintegrated.

In the midst of the crawling, from behind a heap of papers
and magazines, in a room that barely passed as a doctor's office,
a stern-faced Scottish Jew told a teenage girl she was pregnant.
(Better to be shot.)

"And what do you think about that?"

(Think?)

"I try not to." (What am I thinking? He really didn't want to
know.) He sat for a long time studying her face until the foolishness of her self-pitying attitude embarrassed her. She smiled.

"I think it has been a long time since I smiled at a white
man."

"You'll be all right," he said as he patted her shoulder. "Come
back whenever you want to."

Was it he who showed her how to pick up the shards of her
life and re-weave a new fabric? Or was it that he had made her

feel that this was needed and could be done? In the lines of his face and the truth he saw hidden behind the masks she wore, she saw the granny she had left behind.

In the years which unfolded, the world rolled out before my eyes and the dull grey tints that shadowed the colours of my life slowly fell away. In 1979, I saw cherry blossoms bloom bright pink in the glare of a lemon-yellow sun along a street flanked by yards filled with flowers. It seemed like the first time I had ever noticed the flowers. I watched the cherry blossoms bloom on the flushed cheeks of little children, my own and the European children whom they loved. My children, who have never been blinded to themselves or to green fields and purple/gold sunsets, can love Tina Turner, Dolly Parton and Kicking Woman Singers with impunity and a deep sense of equality.

Little Indians (from India), Natives and Europeans can love me and not see Hollywood caricatures of the wrinkled copper skin of my grandmothers. They don't see my grannies, but not because they find me alien—because they simply cannot imagine being that old.

"We will rebuild a nation
ten times more beautiful than before."

"Better make that a minimum
of ten thousand times for North America, Ho."

Returning again to the teachers: Do they begin to understand the magnitude of their impact on the reality we must all go home to face? Do they witness the futility of pedagogy for the chemically seduced little children (whatever their race) of the 1980s? Do they witness the sickening urgency of the children's noonday trek to the corner store for their daily hit of sugar—and do they weep?

Do they know the history of the courageous women healers who organized and protested the production and importation of

sugar to their country almost five hundred years ago? Do they
know that the fate of these women who actively campaigned
against this "poison" was to be burned at the stake for heresy?
The church owned and controlled much of the sugar trade. It
required the traffic of human slaves and a willing population.
Women healers were persecuted for their objections. Did they
teach you that in your history?

It is just a little pathetic that I have to teach you now. I am
less concerned about your distortion of my history than your
inability to hang on to your own.

A cold, grey dawn promised rain on the birthday of my little
daughters' friend. By afternoon, the clouds had been dumping
their excess in earnest. Decked out in bright yellow rubber rain
gear and armed with a present we could ill afford, the pair of
them trudged off braving the elements to join the party. Ah, the
pain on their faces and the silence on their return; the urgency
they must have read in my voice when I asked them why they
were not at the party.

My chubby little moon-faced girl clutched a beleaguered
package whose wrappings the rain had destroyed. It was a long
time before her elder sister threw herself onto the sofa and
wailed, "They told us they didn't want no Indians at the party
and why don't we just go home." Her thin little body sobbed to
the rhythm of the rain. The younger child was too shocked and
outraged to cry.

I could not cry. I dared not be angry. I could not teach my
babies to hate or bow to the cruelty of racism. I undressed them
and held them. David Campbell's beautiful song floated in my
head and I sang:

> Thirty thousand years ago
> Guess who found Ka-Nata?
> No, not Columbus
> Thought he'd reached India

'Twas a little brown man
with an arrow and a bow . . .

We have been forced to reach down inside ourselves to find
the words that will teach our children not to approve of Europeans as they are, but to understand how they came to be and
how they will come to change. We have had to teach our young
to fight for themselves. We have had to figure out a way to create children who can realize their private aspirations no matter
what obstacles the world puts in their paths.

To the rhythm of the rain drumming its timeless song on the
roof of our humble home, my voice softly whispered: "All of
life is the struggle of the living to overcome the obstacles placed
in their pathway as they walk through life. Where life puts no
obstacle, you must create your own. Challenge is the mother of
the seed of brilliance. Overcoming challenge is the flower of
that seed."

We are given this obstacle not by our choice, nor even their
choice. If we overcome it, we can create a new world.

Those who would deny you your humanity have themselves
lost theirs. What a sad thing that the parents of those children
would close the door to their babies' hearts forever by filling
them with such cynicism before they are half grown. Ka-Nata
will stop inflicting pain on our children when we stop bending
and baring our backs to the lash.

And did you see, teachers of my children, the terrible struggle of my small daughters to return to school and face your students with dignity? Did you see the lonely years roll by so
slowly, friendlessly, for my shy and sweet Tania? Did you see
how hard it was for her to move about the school as though she
truly did belong? In your shallow accusation that my second
daughter, Columpa, must be stoned because she seemed
groundlessly happy, was there not just a little racism buried
there?

With a deep sense of loyalty and courage, they sang for you, wrote poetry for you, played music and ran for you. They did not grovel, but neither were they hostile or resentful. Patience won out. Genuine respect came from a few of the students, and my home is filled with the laughter of children of many nationalities. It was my children who led that struggle and won.

9. Heartless Teachers

I KNOW THERE ARE teachers who have been good for my children. I remember one such teacher's words: "Don't you think it would be better if everyone simply looked at one another as people?" I do not remember my impromptu mutterings, but I will write my answer here.

You taught my child that, here, on the West Coast, we were cannibals. I had to tell my daughters that their great-great-granny, who was almost a hundred years old when I was a child, had never eaten a single soul. When I asked her about cannibalism, she said, "My granny never ate anyone. If she had she would have taught me how human flesh is best prepared, for it was her obligation to teach me how best to cook all that our men-folk would eat. The Black Robe I met before this century said his people had been here for a hundred years, but we only knew of them through the great fire that burned all the wood we needed to weave blankets, construct weirs and sew nets. The fire brought hunger; still we ate no one. We died instead, bloated bellies full of air. Of a thousand of us then, we are but a hundred now."

You have always been seen as people in our eyes, but we are still cannibals in yours. What need do you have to insist that we are at best descendants of a distorted people? Until we are also seen as people, we are not equal and there can be no unity between us. Until our separate history is recognized and our need for self-determination satisfied, we are not equal.

You give my children Europe to emulate, respect and learn from, and at the same time, debase Native peoples' national roots. Who is going to insist that Europe's descendants in my homeland learn from and emulate the heroes and bright moments in our history? Which European child in your classroom knows of Khatsalano, Coquitlam, Capilano or our much-lauded (by us) statesman and self-taught constitutional lawyer, Andrew Paull? None of these fine men knew their ancestors to be cannibals, because they never attended your institutions. I might add that Andrew Paull was self-taught because Native men of his time were not permitted to attend law school without renouncing their status as Natives.

Who will teach Europeans that in 1974 an Inuit boy searched the frozen arctic for edible lichens, carefully sharing every morsel with a European man who was so cynical about life that he hoarded and hid from this child food he had found on the plane. He apportioned himself rations of food while this Inuit boy searched for food for both of them. He watched this boy search vainly, for hours each day, on an empty stomach, while his own belly was gratified. He watched him trudge through the frozen snow, braving the wind and cold, until starvation and weakness overcame him and he died. Still, he shared not a morsel of his food. Who will teach your children that the European was never tried for his criminal negligence because of a legal technicality which has never been rectified?

Would this treachery against humanity have gone unpunished had the heroic child been European and the man Inuit? We do not even have to ask the question. We know that they would either have both survived or both died.

What is really pathetic is that this shameless man's mother made excuses for him. She mumbled in a telephone interview about how there was not enough food for both of them. Are our mothers' sons less important than any of your mothers' sons?

My children have mastered their humanity. They have done so because every one of their mothers and their mothers' mothers would have died of shame at such a son. It is without hostility that they offer themselves up for your schooling. But, unlike many of the children in your school, they know about and strive to be like that Inuit boy. He speaks to their ancestry in a way Europe never could. He calls them to attention in a way that your queen and your flag cannot.

We are not awed by his heroism. We are nauseated by the creation of such a warped mind as could watch a child die of starvation while eating, secretly, the only food there was, on the excuse that "there wasn't enough to go around." That we still create such children is living testimony to the real strength and beauty of our grandmothers' words.

"Why can't we be just people?" Do you hear what you say? When did we ever question your right to be considered people? Do you question mine? I know what you think you say. You want me to consider myself not Native, not Cree, not Salish, but a person, absent of nationality or racial heritage. All of us just people, without difference. You fail to see your own hypocrisy. In the same breath, you pick up a guitar and teach European modern folk songs to all the children, but nowhere do European children learn the folk music of my children or any other nationality. Such sameness amounts to everyone's obliteration but your own.

I know we were supposed to have vanished by now. We do not apologize for our inability to do that. Not only are we still here, but some of us are amazingly intact. One hundred years ago General Custer's edict was to kill every man, woman, child and dog at Wounded Knee. To re-word this edict from physical

oblivion to cultural banishment will not soften my natural resistance. I refuse to vanish.

To be fair, ought you not to advocate your own obliteration
before mine? 'Tis not my folk who teach children the sort of
crude individualism that would allow them to starve one of
your children to save their own ass.

In the interest of humanity, you ought to sound the death
knell of your own decadent ways and the renaissance of my
ways. Such things as genocide, confinement and cultural prohibition are not part of my ways. We were almost obliterated by
your ancestors. I realize you hold no gun to my head, dear
teacher, but it was your culture that spawned physical genocide
and now you ask me to erase the shadow of my grandmother.
Before you ask me to erase her, please reduce yourself to a
shadow. Then, we will at least be equal. At base zero, I am willing to negotiate a whole new culture, if you like. Otherwise,
keep your offensive words locked in your narrow mind.

10. L'ilwat Child

I WAS ON A BUS heading back to the school. We were returning from another of my children's field trips with their classmates. I was volunteering because my children wanted me to. Don't mistake me, I love all children—at first. But through the years of volunteering for school field trips, I have become very concerned about the child-rearing skills of North American parents. I have had to referee some very serious violent outbursts between children. Not the sort of violence of the '50s, when children occasionally pulled each other's hair or knocked each other down. I mean fights with both feet and fists-a-flying, weapons of wood and metal employed. I have heard foul language such as I never heard on the docks of the Steveston slums.

Today looked like it was going to be different from other field trips. There had not been a fight. There were three little girls seated across from me on the trip. Two little European girls and one dark, black-eyed L'ilwat child. A pretty little girl. No one spoke to her. I hoped that that was because she was new to the school. On the return trip the teacher instructed the

children to sit in their original seats. The little L'ilwat girl got on
the bus in that slow deliberate way we have of walking. The two
little European girls took up the entire seat and sat whispering
to each other. They did not move. The L'ilwat girl waited
politely and patiently for them to move. Stubbornly mute, they
sat still while the teacher was reduced to shouting threats and
finally physically moved them to one side so that the little L'ilwat girl would have room to sit. Even then, the two girls
resisted moving any more than the bare minimum to enable the
girl to sit half on the seat.

No comfort was offered to the dark-eyed child. No apologies
to the insulted girl were asked for or offered. It was as though
the answer to the question "Do Indians have feelings?" was a
categorical "No." It was the teacher's authority that was asserted
and not the child's right to a seat.

Our children can expect no more than a seat in the class-
rooms of the nation. No dignity, and certainly we cannot expect
friendship. What about the United Nations Charter and a
child's right to dignity? Don't educators know that Canada
signed that Charter? When will you teach your children that
mine, too, must be accorded respect?

The little girl had been through this before. A mask of
infinite nothingness covered her face. The same mask we all had
to wear at one time or another. My insides wanted to scream. I
reached down deep: "Grandmothers, put your timeless loving
selves . . ." I am ashamed now. I let the scream sink slowly into
oblivion. I went home to scream my rage to a blank sheet of
paper. I had not moved to comfort that child either. I betrayed
myself yet again.

For my hungry, aching spirit, the pen is mightier than the
sword. The agony of our young will have to be endured yet
another generation. 'Tis not we who must be asked to treat others as human beings. Europe has much to learn from our example. Be ever so thankful that I have not forgotten my ancestors
and looked upon myself as just a person or I would have

exploded in good European style on those children. I ought to have slapped them both.

Locked in your white-skinned privilege and blinded by your arrogance, you call on me to forget the past and be like you. You know not what you ask. If I forget my past, ignore our ancient ways, only violence will quiet the scream inside me.

Despite all my grandmother's efforts, I am still a crippled two-tongued slave, not quite an ex-Native. I still feel a great need to address you, to try and alter you—to humanize you. The colour of betrayal is honey-brown, over top a white mind, skin stretched taut with the need to prove we are human. The colour of betrayal is bright yellow for the cowardice and the complacency I always manage to come up with when my eyes see bright red rage.

Trapped in a cage of shame, we lash out at each other and spare you. You mention the Black Panther Party and its violence. Thirty-seven Black community leaders were killed by white police and one white person killed by the party. Who was hurt? Twenty years later, the party is dead and the life of Black people is shorter for that fact. More Blacks were killed last year by other Blacks than the death toll during the entire decade of the Irish-English war. And Native people are not so far behind. Three-quarters of the Native inmates of federal penitentiaries are there for violence against other Native people.

Why? Betrayal. The Black Panther Party believed you and your liberal brothers when they were told, "We are all just people." Worse. They didn't love themselves. "Black and White Unite!" was the call, but who knew then that erasure of Black people was the terms of unity? We should have known. Nothing had changed for North America. No revolution has occurred since its bloody birth more than two hundred years ago. We doubted each other when we believed you.

The terms you offer me are the same. Disappear, disappear. Do you think me shameless or stupid? The price of denying my grandmother is neglecting my children.

As a ragged, battle-worn teenager—the only "injun" in my class—I did try to deny my own heritage. I donned the sacred mantle of self-centred individualism, the heart and spirit of Canadian achievement, and stumbled through my studies. I dressed in blue serge skirts and painted my face with Mabeline and I even cut my hair. I grabbed hold of doors I never knew were locked. "Go to university," was the clarion call. "Anyone can get through." On a cold wintry dawn, amid white death and fallen logs, I locked the door myself.

In my grade eleven History class each student was required to read from the text each day. When the teacher called my turn, I glanced at the clean white page with black characters all over it. "Louis Riel was a madman who was hanged . . ." I could not buy that any more than I could the cannibalism fairytale of fifth grade. I could not forsake my ancestors for all your students to see. The coldness of not caring is more deadly than an Arctic storm.

I hope the words "integrate into European society" dribble meaninglessly from your lips, because if you understand their meaning then truly you are a ridiculous caricature of humanity. You seek to "renew us; to remake us; to make us perfect, whole." Get away from my face. We are not half-human, in need of remodelling. It sickens my spirit to have to address your madness, but you stand in front of my people, and to speak to each other, we must first rid ourselves of you. Our inability to move, to strive, is born of a great reluctance to be debauched slaves in your image. It is the source of our great strength.

> The educators in my life led me
> to my own desertion.
> The colour of betrayal is grey.
> There are no flowers
> in a traitor's life
> no violet-red sun,
> just rain
> grey concrete and cloudy days.

You delude yourself that my only complaint centres on the ignorant remarks of your helpless children, who berate mine for their Indian-ness. Do you think I could condemn your poisoned children for your crimes? No, my fellow educators, the rotten stench of racism permeates this entire land and lives quite healthily in your living rooms. Every nook and cranny in this country is filled with its foul air. Educators are the primary thrust of racism, the front line of soldiers in the battle to eradicate all that is not Anglo-Saxon and Protestant. I condemn not children. You will have to take responsibility for your world and the education of its citizenry.

The desire of our people to gain a foothold in this society is arrogantly interpreted as a desire to be like Europeans. We have never feared or rejected new things, new knowledge. But quite frankly, we do not respect the ways of European CanAmerica. We seek knowledge that we may turn it to our own use. Do not be surprised when I tell you that your knowledge is not the only knowledge we seek.

11. *Education*

WHEN OUR GRANDMOTHERS sent their children to school it was with self-sufficiency and mastery over the production of new things in mind. They did not realize that we would never be taught to create iron cooking pots from the ore of the earth. Our third generation is being educated in the European system and our children know less about the production of the stuff of life than did our grandmothers. Schools have shown themselves to be ideological processing plants, turning out young people who cannot produce the means to sustain themselves, but who are full of the ideological nonsense of European culture.

We have learned something in the last two decades. We have learned that to change things will require tremendous power, and that we lack power. We are going to acquire it in the same fashion that we lost it, tenaciously and doggedly. We are going to pursue empowerment.

And don't point at the new crew of Native teachers who have been processed in the same fashion as all the other teachers, as an example for me to follow. Many of these teachers have good intentions and pledge their allegiance to establishing separate schools with Native content in the curriculum for Native children. The dismal failure of Canadian schools is obvious, but the redress needed may not be merely segregation. Segregated schools alone will not change the basic historical pattern of colonialism; only decolonization will do that.

Adding a sprinkling of our culture to European parasitic culture is offensive, particularly in the absence of an understanding of our laws and the philosophy that underlies them. To spice the ideology of exploitation, individualism and middle-class aspiration with the emptied art-forms and stripped songs of the ancients, is to reduce ourselves to a joke. Tradition is useful only insofar as it allows us to continue to make use of our history.

To whine about the destruction of our language and customs, without trying to come to grips with the reasons for the destruction, is pure mental laziness. The appropriation of knowledge, its distortion and, in some cases, its destruction, were vital to the colonial process. The conqueror relies on his victims for obeisance. The culture of the conqueror is justified by the notion that some sort of "godly" or inherent right to conquer belongs solely to him. Colonialism has racism as its ideological rationale. We must fundamentally alter the relations of the colonial system; to dress our enslavement in Native garb is useless. We need to reclaim our essential selves, engage ourselves as the cultural, spiritual, emotional and physical beings we were and march forward, laying to rest one hundred years of cultural prohibition and arrest.

Armed with the skills of language and possessing the privilege of access to all the knowledge secreted in these institutions of higher learning, you would think that our educated heroes would investigate our history. It seems the farther we go in these processing plants, the more we leave ourselves behind.

The first thing a would-be Native educator ought to come to grips with is the function of education. It is not to become successful. Success is the by-product of what knowledge a person applies to life; it is the satisfactory achievement of something. Too often success is seen as synonymous with wealth, useful employment or a regular salary.

It is the function of systematic education and training to promulgate the knowledge and culture of a given society in the context of a given historical perspective. That perspective is always determined by who has the power. The culture of this society is based on the rape and plunder of the nations it has conquered. It serves the interests of a few elite corporate entities, which are the sources of power and authority. The means to produce life does not exist solely within the borders of this society. Much of our clothing, electronic equipment, food, etc., comes from former colonies which are financially dependent on North America. That is the simple premise which Native teachers mis-educated by Europeans cannot deal with, without a gentle nudge from below. But deal with it we must.

Once we understand what kind of world they have created, then we can figure out what kind of world we can re-create. We need not worry how much or how little that new world is culturally Native. It is next to impossible to destroy culture without annihilating the people. The Beothuk culture of Newfoundland is definitely a dead culture by virtue of the fact that there are not any living Beothuks in the world.

I am bone weary of the new Native educators (and, for that matter, the Native lawyers) who prate about including our view of history in the textbooks. I can just see the way such a text would read. "Madman/spiritual leader Louis Riel massacred/ defeated white settlers/the enemy at Duck Lake today." Or better yet, they are going to say that our ancestors "made a great contribution to the development of Canada." This implies that our grandmothers helped build colonialism as much as white folk did. Not my grandmother; she taught me to be loyal to myself and to our folk. At least she tried to.

A new history will only be written by those who would

change the course of history. There is no other way, short of re-instituting segregated schooling. To have one point of view for settler and Native, you must have unity between them.

Education is all about maintaining culture. In this country there is no need for children to be taught any practical skills. Very few of the educated children of this country will actually produce an object of utility or design the objects we use in our lives. Science, mathematics, health are all taught in the abstract, with no relation to practice. It is ridiculous that children don't acquire the practical training necessary to participate in the productive life of society until they are adults.

The first twelve years of instruction children receive amount to fixing up their heads so that they will move without complaint according to the way society is organized. The society we live in is racist. Naturally, the education we receive is racist. Our students are the victims of this racism. It takes a tremendous amount of effort on the part of Native parents and our children to prevent racism from becoming internalized.

The conditions of life of white people in Canada are much better than those of our people. White students cannot help but be aware of this. Our children know it. They are taught that this is our own fault: that we are inferior lunkheads, or, in a more sophisticated vein, that logic and science are not concepts we can readily deal with. White students have no basis for according us respect, so they don't. To ask our students to hold themselves up under the biting lash of racism is criminal. To ask our students to forget the past is to negate their present. The present they enjoy is not disconnected from their past.

As mature adults, we are responsible for cleaning up the mess in which we historically have allowed ourselves to become enmeshed. Responsible: having the ability to respond to a given situation. (This has nothing to do with laying blame.) We must respond to our conditions of life in order to change them. This change does not amount to taking the same old story and putting the words in the mouths of brown faces to be properly parroted by them. It amounts to finding a way to loosen the grip that colonialism has on us.

In the process of trying to free ourselves, we will learn. Change must be the basis for education and cultural development. It begins with learning. Learning begins with objectifying our condition and the condition of our homeland. To learn "how we are to live among them" does not mean that we should segregate ourselves from or subordinate ourselves to them. It means that we must build a new society based on the positive histories of both. A critical examination of the history of settler society is in order. Likewise, a critical examination of our society is in order.

We have not "lost our culture" or had it "stolen." Much of the information that was available to us through our education process has been expropriated and consigned to deadwood leaves in libraries. The essence of Native culture still lives in the hearts, minds and spirits of our folk. Some of us have forsaken our culture in the interest of becoming integrated. That is not the same thing as losing something. The expropriation of the accumulated knowledge of Native peoples is one legacy of colonization. Decolonization will require the repatriation and the rematriation of that knowledge by Native peoples themselves.

12. *The Rebel*

CONQUEST AND CONTINUED domination require force, an organized force of occupation. The persecution and destruction of all forms of resistance—physical, cultural and political—is the duty of that army. Laws against us are made for these armed thugs to uphold. Whether resistance takes the form of individual or social rebellion, it must be suppressed. Laws are constructed by the occupying force to facilitate the suppression of any resistance from the dominated people. Such things as justice and other nebulous concepts have nothing to do with maintaining power. The laws of this country are unequal, force upholds them and justice is foreign to their very formulation.

Destruction and expropriation of knowledge, particularly language, medicine (science) and culture, is a prerequisite for the unabated persecution of pockets of resistance. The aims of the colonizer are to break up communities and families, and to destroy the sense of nationhood and the spirit of co-operation among the colonized. A sense of powerlessness is the legacy handed down to the colonized people. Loss of power—the

negation of choice, as well as legal and cultural victimization—
is the hoped-for result. It can never be wholly achieved.

At every juncture in the history of colonization, we have
resisted domination. Each new prohibition was met with
defiance, overt and covert. What else would you call "night-
fishing"? Some of the defiance was organized. We still resist. In
the Stein Valley, on the Queen Charlotte Islands, on Meares
Island, patriots are resisting the wholesale, wanton destruction
of our homeland. These people are the authors of a new society.
The Okanagan as a tribal group helped to effect a moratorium
on uranium mining; they will do so again should the provincial
government lift the moratorium. The Gitksan-Wet'suwet'en are
opposed to massive clear-cutting of the forest as the only means
to employment in their homeland. They are not completely dismissive of logging, but clear-cutting is not the only method of
securing logs.

Those who would re-write history from the closets of settler
institutions instead of with their feet firmly rooted in resistance
are not rebels. Rebels don't generally go to school. They resist,
culturally, by withdrawing from the schools that would "fix"
their heads. Rebels don't play at re-writing history; they make
history by taking to the streets, peacefully at times, violently at
times, but always in paramilitary style—conscious that it is a
fight to the finish. While the educated Natives sit in comfy,
respectable kitchens, amicably discussing the historical options
open to our people and trying to conceive of the best possible
deal they can finagle from the State on our behalf, the rebels are
honing their knives in joyous anticipation of the final day of
reckoning.

We are not a violent people, but neither are we fools. Those
not befogged by the obscure phrase-mongering of the oppressor
are sharply aware of their condition. They know they must
fight. If they sit in the bars in vain attempts to drown their
fighting spirit, it is because they are not sure how they are to

fight and win. It is our history of losing that keeps us locked to the bar stools, not our fear of fighting.

To most of the elite, re-writing our history is equal to digni-fied betrayal. To the rebel, altering her condition will re-write her life onto the pages of a new history. Only rebellion, the spir-itual cleansing of the bad blood that separates her from her womanhood, can appease the rebel. But we need to know that we can win.

Fighting the good fight used to be good enough. There is in the spirit of people a truth that lingers in the atmosphere that shrouds our community; the sense that this last fight is the deci-sive one. If we don't win this one we are a lost people—a dead people. This desperation is the harbinger of brutal violence directed at ourselves. Poised taut, eager for the good fight, but immobilized by the ominous power of the State and the confu-sion sown by the elite, everyone becomes a traitor or a cow-ard—mirroring our own paralysis. We fight each other.

To win we must plan in the cellars and attics, lurking in the dark with one eye cast about for the enemy. In our heart of hearts, we know the enemy is a beast that will stop at nothing to keep his world intact. We know that his money comes to him "dripping from every pore with the blood and toil of millions." We know the enemy is ever watchful, on guard day and night against the potential threat we all pose. To plan, we must learn to sum up our history—not the history of betrayal but the his-tory of our resistance. We must learn from our mistakes and chart the course for our eventual victory.

We must also understand and cherish the history of ordinary white folk—the history of their victimization and their resis-tance. It is true that a man will work anywhere to support his family. White and Native men work in the fish camps that deplete the fish stock, in the forests where they clear-cut the logs, but they do not own the corporations that profit by the rape of the land and sea. These corporate marauders don't care a tinker's damn for their own folk any more than they care for us, the land or the fish.

The initial upsurge of politicized youth in the 1960s was a chaotic one. It was dominated by disenchanted students who, given the dream, were angered by the reality of racism that prevented them from realizing the dream. They objected to the injustice. In the groundswell, those of us who had always worked to survive had no delirious dreams of a better, more comfortable life under the settler's heel. We sought not the silk sheets of continued domination, but rather dared to want the unreasonable: independence.

We rose up alongside the intelligentsia, eager to learn and anxious to fight. Our bare arms, raw muscle and spirit of resistance were all we had.

We didn't think much about the demands of the intellectuals. We did not think about our own aspirations. In fact, many of us did not know what our dreams were: "I just wanted to fight." We assumed that the intellectuals were smarter than we were, and, even more dangerously, that they embraced common desires. The words of the intellectuals came alive for us, breathed new life into our bent and tired bodies, and gave us the power to think thoughts and dream dreams. We loved them. We followed the direction that they alluded to—right down one blind alley after another. But we learned.

There is power in knowing. Our thirst for knowledge partially slaked, we drove forward always active, always looking again, until a seemingly insurmountable mountain pass was reached and only a fresh new perspective would get us over it, a perspective rooted in our own people's knowledge. The law of the people and the code of conduct that was so important to our ancestors was what we needed.

We found that intellectuals preferred the truth with its clothes on. They preferred polite discussion about abstract ideas and not the challenge that characterized our old ways. They preferred peace—at any price—to the inevitable consequences of social resistance. They feared the wrath of the State. The rage of backlash from white folk terrified the intelligentsia. "We don't want to alienate our white supporters" was the hue and cry of these pampered babies. Divorced from their communities, alienated from their culture, they preferred distorted recognition by white liberal supporters rather than the mass movement of Native youth.

I am not so cynical as to believe that white people will withdraw their support if we seek to have equal relations based on truth. White supporters have never demanded that we subordinate ourselves in the interest of unity. Those who are appalled by our insistence on self-determination were never our supporters. They only held out the promise of support in exchange for the subordination of our interests. There is a big difference.

In 1969, a growing division in the movement between Red Power activists and orthodox leaders was hastened by the government's creation of "official" organizations replete with employed bureaucrats and heavy injections of money. Most of the dollars have gone to consultants and lawyers who happen to be white. In the absence of clear aims and objectives for a viable alternative which could oppose these organizations, the youth power movement defended its legitimacy through its mass action. It was already moribund. More and more people began to see that the organizations could achieve social reform more effectively and much more rapidly through the "proper channels."

Steadily, with cruel relentlessness, the youth movement dwindled and lost initiative. Many of the youth sought consolation in drugs and alcohol or hired themselves out to the big organizations. Confusion followed. For those who no longer wished to be identified with mass civil disobedience, cultural nationalism became the convenient flag to hide behind. On the ebb of the tide, dead wood washes out to sea.

It was time to study the reasons for the receding tide. What had been a great blossoming of youth turned into paralysis and demoralization. Desertion to the ranks of the organizations was widespread. In the midst of this, State-paid would-be healers, spiritual leaders, rose to show the way. In the absence of a real struggle, a caricature will do.

The big organizations—conservative, steeped in bureaucracy and dependent on government funds as they were—did not do anything that was not within the guidelines established by the funding sources. As the money poured in the guidelines became more stringent. The opposition from the leaders was polite— they were disempowered. The staff of the organizations was drawn from among the most astute and active youth who were thoroughly mis-educated by the settler's institutions of higher learning. The price of receiving a good job was undying loyalty to the leadership. The politics of self-government was restricted to regional and tribal autonomy and to joint corporate economic development.

The rebel youth were aware of the sell-out character of the officially recognized leadership. This awareness was not based on a careful examination of the essential character of the organizations, their philosophy, ideology or their policies. It was an emotional response to the personal conduct of the individuals and leaders within the organizations. To gain the loyalty of the youth they needed only to "clean up their act."

In 1973, at the juncture of the lowest ebb in the movement, the Wounded Knee siege broke out. The American Indian Movement was propelled to the fore of the siege by a biased and sensationalist press. The most vocal and articulate males, those who conducted themselves the most like arrogant white men, were interviewed and reported on over and over again. Touted as leaders, these men overshadowed the issue. The real goals of the occupation were lost in the shuffle. The leadership clique entrenched itself. These leaders began to hire themselves out for speaking tours, initially to raise money for the Wounded Knee trials. Later they began to live off the movement rather than for it.

The American Indian Movement began as a street patrol,

fashioned after the Black Panther Party, in much the same way that other Native militant groups were. Even concepts of local chapters, national chairmen and mass recruitment into the organization were similar to the Black Panther Party's style of organizing. The politics were no different either. Culturally, the worst, most dominant white male traits were emphasized. Machismo and the boss mentality were the basis for choosing leaders. This idea of leadership was essentially a European one promulgated by power mongers.

Over time, the AIM leaders denied the validity of political struggle. Their method of leadership was to ignore and alienate any and all internal opposition. In fact, the historical destiny of AIM's leadership was to bandage the wounds of a few Native people with a bigger share of the pie—in the name of independence. (I, here, leave out the 1975 convention in which John Trudell was elected.) Self-imposed leaders, bolstered by white liberals and the white media, deserved the lion's share of the pie.

Passive resistance is our chief enemy. Instead of thrashing it out with the leadership, we went away. "It wasn't worth it," the disenchanted rebels murmured. It took a long time for us to look beyond conduct, to see that it was based on character. Character is in turn based on philosophy. Philosophy is the key to culture.

Inherent in a people's philosophy is the sense of logic that allows them to see the internal relationships governing them. That logic guides their conduct, their governing structures and their mode (way) of organizing far more surely than their vision of the future. We may all have a common goal, but the way we organize to achieve that goal will determine the results more surely than the goal itself. We all desired independence. Those of us who locked the door from the inside of the gravy train and those who would not climb the steps to board the train all wanted independence.

The problem was that we were all motivated by personal survival. In the absence of the inherent logic of our philosophy, the

survival of official organizations seemed to be founded on pre-
determined Canadian legalism. Natives who had already
adopted the Canadian forms of organization established Native
para-civil service bureaucracies. They had already decided that
the basis for their conduct would be rooted in Canadian culture.
We had no way to move beyond survival and retrieve our own
way of conducting ourselves in modern organizations rooted in
our past cultural context.

Likewise, the AIM leadership looked at the rewards of "serv-
ing the people" with European eyes. Their interpretation of
spirituality was rooted in European culture. Their inability
to accept criticism from below and opposition from across the
table, and to alter their conduct accordingly, rendered their
leaders impotent.

For some of us, the arithmetic of salaried leadership was
revolting. The salaries seemed enormous. Indians could not pay
for such leadership; thus, salaried leaders were not working for
us, but for someone else. For many youth, being employed by
"the enemy" was deterrent enough.

For AIM, the orthodox leaders and the United States govern-
ment-paid tribal councils were sell-outs. (Not because the form
of organization, the methods of leadership and the philosophical
view of the tribal councils reflected the U.S. government, but
because they accomplished too little too late.) Power politics
does work. Concessions were fought for and won. Independence is paid for with people's lives. Social movement alone can
bring America to its senses. And there is no doubt that America
can be brought to its senses.

AIM did not challenge the basic character or the legitimacy of
the institutions or even the political and economic organization
of America; rather, it addressed the long-standing injustice of
expropriation. Russell Means attempted, by a series of incorrect
historical acrobatics, to "prove" that Europeans were hopeless.
The result was a biased treatise against the only European rebels
in history—the Marxists. It is one thing to defend the rights of

Native people to relate to white people as equals. It is quite another to attack the rebels as enemies. It is rather repulsive to falsify the history of an entire people for the purpose of launching an attack on the system's rebels. It is just so much narcissism to do so in the name of your own "correct peoples."

There is a hair-splitting and negligible difference between the racism and national "my country, willy nilly" chauvinism of America and the "correct peoples" philosophy of Russell Means. We all had the same beginning. The fork in the road was at the juncture of conduct, that great cultural separator, rooted in the philosophical logic of two separate peoples. In our world today there are only two points of view: the view of the colonizer and the view of those who would effect liberation. The colonizer is not a rebel. He does not come from the ranks of ordinary white men.

The logic of the colonizer for the last five centuries has been and continues to be "How can I turn this to my advantage?" The logic of the colonized is "How can we turn this around so that we can regain our lost sense of humanity?" There are those among us who have filled themselves with the settler's logic. It allows certain Natives to live off the movement instead of living for it.

There is no European substitute for our own philosophical premise for being: "spirit is life-force—essence." All things—stone, earth, flora, fauna (of which people are a small part)—are alive with their own spirit and reason for being. This premise puts us all on the same level. To articulate this premise without conducting oneself as though it were true is to be comfortable with one's hypocrisy in the same way that middle-class Can-America is generally comfortable with its hypocrisy.

We all wanted independence and none of us quite knew what that was. We travelled down one blind alley after another, while a busy, huge and moneyed corporate elite went into operation to smash us. They organized us into offices replete with all the machinery and power and respectability hitherto denied us;

then, they paid us. For those like the leaders of AIM, who could not accept direct salaries from government, a host of angels came to the rescue. The stars, rich liberals and the church offered their insidious charity. The media attention brought in the dollars that gave leadership mobility and its reason for being.

Conduct itself is not enough. Those who were inspired by the raw courage of the early days of AIM (its audacious power-politics approach), were ill-equipped to come to grips with the basis of its leadership's misconduct. For some, drugs, booze and suicide provided a route out of the darkness of demoralization. Others gave up their principles and tied themselves to the organizations where they hoped to change the conduct of the leadership from within.

I confess that I am an intellectual. I was at one time dismissive of this class but have since realized that, stuck within it as I am, alone with but a half-dozen "radicals" who are also attacked by this class, I am lonely. I want to be seen, heard and remembered. Most of all, I want to make a little mark on the historical destination of Native people. I did not escape self-interested motivation any more than those I criticize. I want you, the reader, to adopt the slogan "one must doubt everything" when you read this or any other book.

The intellectual class has done everything it can to stop me from having voice. With the help of a few well-placed and powerful white bureaucrats, my name has been besmirched by rumours and slanderous attacks. In much the same way that the vast majority of the people in North America find all that is not asinine, mundane and dreary, "weird," in this way do my colleagues decry me. I expect it from government and white liberals, but not from my own colleagues. Self-pity is ugly but for a time it was my crutch. This book is all about the inside of me. It is all about my insight. I hardly think it fair to lay bare my insights to my colleagues and withhold the truth from myself.

There is nothing worse than being a woman who is dark, brilliant and déclassée. Darkness is the absence of natural (normal?) class polish. Admit this, all of you. I laugh too loud, can't hold my brownie properly in polite company and am apt to call shit "shit." I can't be trusted to be loyal to my class. In fact, the very clever among the elite know that I am opposed to the very existence of an elite among us. For me, the struggle for self-determination will end with the dissolution of this elite and the levelling of the CanAmerican class structure or it will continue—for a thousand years if need be.

You have acquired your knowledge, friends, through the spoils of a colonial system which intends to use you to oppress my poor country-cousins. I owe no apology for refusing to go along with that.

The difference between myself and the new middle-class Natives is that I came by my knowledge through a great need to change. I needed to change. I was so fucked up. I cannot sit on my ass in fat, second-hand leather chairs still warm from the cheeks of some departing white bureaucrat's butt. I really hope I keep the elite awake at night. If one of them thinks hard enough to realize the folly of following CanAmerica to the edge of disaster, then the pain of writing this book will have been worth it.

There are precious few intellectuals who have not internalized the adage that the best direction is a European one. There are a few, though, and our impact on history will be great.

The preceding words provide the context for my personal examination of the power-politics movement of the 1960s. I am familiar with the events because I was very much a part of that movement. Few writers are willing to state their personal feelings about things before subjecting things to the cold light of analysis. I do not believe any opinion is free of bias and the preceding words reflect my particular biases. What follows are my conclusions and a summation of the situation that urban Natives find themselves in.

The mass character and pure idealism of the movement were killed by the reality of the power of the State: murder for those who could not be bought or beaten; jail for those too popular to kill and for whom the possibility of breaking the spirit existed; isolation for those who could be isolated. Apathy, and a great reluctance to be misled, yet again, led to mass integration, at least on the surface level.

The last fifteen years have been characterized by the birth of a large and stable urban population. In the past a great number of us came to the city, stayed a short while and went home—transient youth moving back and forth between "home" and the city. Our opting for the city as a home was an indication of the road we really wanted to take.

13. *Party Down!*

THE TRANSIENT CHARACTER of the urban community has changed and with it comes the incumbent cultural integration into the oppressor society. The internalization of Canadian culture came harmlessly enough. Party down! The infamous party culture began a short time after the government-funded Native political organizations came into being. Money—excess money—hotel rooms and boogie culture began at the top and filtered down to the masses. It was not that we never partied before. It was the way we did it that changed.

In the communities, celebrations involved everyone—old and infant, youth and middle aged. It was a great coming together of all the people. These celebrations were only mildly encumbered by over-indulgence in alcohol and occasionally they were marred by violence. At least we were together. In the urban centre, families were separated by the new settler-style party. Kids were dumped at baby-sitters and elders were unwelcome and uninvited to the new soirées. Brothers didn't party in the same spot as sisters.

In the city a good party was one in which no kids, old

people or close family were present. That little step changed our social being. No occasion was necessary to give rise to a party. No special event was even desirable. The rest is history. This was the fertile soil in which AIM could plant its seed, flourish and flower. The flower was neither lovely nor sturdy. In fact, it was barren, unable to produce new seeds.

Leaders were not selected on the basis used by our ancestors: selflessness, wisdom, courage and responsiveness to the interests of the people. Instead, verbosity, arrogance and arbitrariness became the standards for selection. The media and white liberals became the judges. People paid for the pearls cast them by the power-politics leaders. Soon, the contact files of movement Natives were top-heavy with white liberals and barren of Native people.

A few of us launched a struggle to reconnect with our old communities. We analyzed how we got bogged down in "big splash" media-mongering politics, and we cross-referenced all mail, throwing out all contacts that we thought were white. This last measure may seem a little absurd, since independence is a question of social relations, not of race. However, it was important as the first step toward relying on our own people.

The sense of drama and the spirit of power that this gave rise to altered the course of political development for us. It freed our minds. Independent thinking was possible. To be critical of all and doubt everything is the first step to the creation of new thought. We were forced to look inside ourselves for the answers and not assume that if you are white you are right. In the long run, it enabled us to be objective about ourselves.

Without the stifling anchors of liberalism, we were able to grow. We published our thoughts in a newsletter with a refreshingly new analysis. "Bread, Brothers and Co-optation"; "The North: Canada's Last Frontier"; and "Neo-colonialism, the Highest Stage of Capitalism" were articles of note during the period. These articles formed the ideological basis for a new and different approach to left-wing politics in North America.

We attempted to organize a liberation movement from the ranks of militants left over from the Red Power movement. The challenge was far too long-range and serious for the burgeoning youth who sought to become part of the elite. The movement was made up largely of students and would-be intellectuals. Faced with organizing a genuinely nationalist movement for our liberation, sell-out politics did not look so bad. In the end, a single veteran clung tenaciously to the politics of anti-imperialism and national liberation and locked herself to a typewriter that drove her poetic aspirations into the public eye years later. Others died in despair. Still others, immobilized, gripped by the impossibility of their vision, retreated to the private world of the depressed.

The American Indian Movement brought a strange sort of corruption and immorality to our militant youth. The activists became branded with the opportunist, hustle-media politics that characterized the movement of the '70s. Sexism, racism's younger brother, was inherent in the character of the American Indian Movement.

14. *Another Side of Me*

THE ASPECT OF the movement which is under constant attack, even by people who know little or nothing about it, is the communist element. I am most sensitive about this aspect for within it lies the kernel of truth of my own political vision.

Native students of leftist politics that grew out of the '60s deserved some of the criticism that people raised. Our communism had both feet rooted in European labour history. In this country, that history is an inglorious one. The foundation of unions here was rooted in racism.

Marx himself was full of arrogance and racial supremacist attitudes; that does not negate his sense of history nor his science of revolution. Revolution! Even the most patriotic militants balk at the word. That the European labour movement was built on our backs, that the workers of this land have always had us as a cushion to soften the blow of recession is undeniable. That white Marxists, communists and would-be leftists are tainted with racism is equally undeniable. But to renounce the principles of communism because its adherents are flawed is absurd.

Marxism is founded on the expropriated knowledge and principles of our old societies, which were handed to Marx in distorted fashion. Coloured by the bias of the church, Marx's research was hindered by the brothel-tinted sunglasses of the clergy. The settlers of this country began life with a lie. They cannot carry the truth of communist theory to fruition. Marx was sensitive to the limitations of his theory. He was sensitive to the colonial reality of capitalism's beginning. He was also very sensitive about the basic reactionary character of those sectors of the labour movement that were racist. He must spin over in his grave once a day at the behaviour of his flagbearers.

Our most brilliant movement leaders have been Native Marxists. Against all odds, they have courageously fought to analyze our history so that we could alter it. Marx died, hungry and ill, struggling to synthesize the lessons of world history, that the history of the world might change. He took his knowledge of the people of the world and found the thread with which we might weave a whole new social fabric. All we needed was the courage to turn around: to make revolution.

That white people are unable to make revolution without our assistance—to turn around the society they created—does not negate the necessity and inevitability of turning it around. It has been my experience that those who are rabidly anti-communist are themselves parasites. They live off the movement. They live off the toil of others.

Revolution means to turn around. Square boxes do not turn around. Circles do. This society is made up of a hierarchical system of classes: rectangles that pile up on one another, with the smallest rectangle and the fewest members at the top of the pyramid. The majority fit into the rectangle at the base. The thinking of the people in this country is married to that reality. It is stratified, linear and racist.

Every time Native people form a circle they turn around. They move forward, not backward into history. We don't have to "go back to the land." We never left it. We are not reptiles or

amphibians that lived in the sea and now wish to go back to the
land. Critics of communism cling to the delusion that the cities
we now inhabit do not exist on land. Innocently, some of the
people that left their original communities feel this way too.
Such thinking is promoted by those who wish to throw the
movement into reverse.

Along with the mistaken notion of land, comes the distortion
of traditionalism. We are and always have been culturally Cree,
Salish, Nis'ga'a and so forth. One does not lose culture. It is not
an object. Culture changes, sometimes for the better, sometimes
for the worse, but it is constantly changing and will do so as
long as people busy themselves with living. Culture is a living
thing. It grows and stagnates by turns. The philosophical
premise of a people rarely alters itself fundamentally, however.
The cultural expression of philosophy may change, but to alter
the foundations takes a great deal more effort than simple legal
prohibition.

Certainly the prohibitive laws surrounding language and cultural expression were both painful and damaging for our cultural initiative. This is unarguable. We now are paralyzed
with fear at cultural innovation. The basis for this fear is the
inequitable relations inherent in colonialism. Let's just think
about how the Salish came by quillwork: by trading with other
Native people. We did not fear this new cultural innovation.
Why? Because we were equals. The trade is indeed a trade;
moccasins for dried fish, so to speak. However, when we adopt
the guitar and country-style music, then we get a little nervous.
Likewise with European philosophy.

Cultural imperialism means altering a colonized people's cultural expression without consideration for the aspirations of the
people. Fortunately, this does not occur with the degree of
thoroughness desired by the imperialists. Even while we use the
medium of European-style music, we infuse our own language,
our own words and our own meaning. Floyd Westerman is a
country singer, but "Custer Died for Your Sins" will not likely

be sung by white country singers for some time to come. It is a song that is culturally ours.

If a culture does not express the conditions, the aspirations and the dreams of a people at any period in their history, then it is a dead culture. Culture is a mirror of a people's way of life. We now live not in longhouses or tipis, but in townhouses and apartment blocks. We purchase our food from a grocery store (though given the condition of the food that is sold at these grocery stores, I am not sure this is a good innovation).

No people ever totally deserts its ancestry. The actual ceremonies of the past, the manner in which they were conducted is a matter of speculation by white anthropological experts. There are few elders alive who were not raised in the tradition of the Catholic church, who were not influenced in some fashion by early colonialism. The ceremonies of those spiritual leaders are, likewise, a matter of personal conjecture.

There is no problem with that. Anything that brings people closer to themselves is a ceremony. The search for the truth of one's spirit is a private one, rich in ceremony. The manner in which a person seeks the self is always based on the sacred right of choice.

The question of the existence of a "Great Spirit" is one that is personal and not the basis of our philosophy. Religion and the manner in which a person resolves their own morality, code of conduct, principles, etc., is based on the laws governing choice. As we all know, communists are self-avowed atheists. They are purported to persecute religious people the world over. Native communists have been patient beyond reason with the religious beliefs of others while being persecuted by those who accuse them of persecution.

The extent to which we cannot tolerate communists, Christians and Buddhists in our midst is the exact measure of our integration into the negative aspects of European culture. The principles of communism regarding religion are simple: everyone has the right to worship and conversely, all have the right to oppose worship—peacefully. No one has the right to use religion to exploit others. Communists do not budge on the question of persecution for the purpose of exploitation. This is most annoying for parasites. The American Indian Movement hates communists.

I firmly believe that the philosophy of my ancestors lines up quite tidily with the philosophy of communism. I make no apology for my principles. What I hold myself to account for is not having fought hard and long for the principles that I hold dear to my heart. I should have thrashed the opponents of anti-communist treachery long ago and didn't. Not because I was afraid of the consequences, but rather because I loved some of the people influenced by anti-communist bogeymen. These are some of the "terrible" principles of communism to which I ascribe:

- End the unequal and oppressive relations between European and Third World Nations.
- End the violent competition between nations of exploiters. Work for peace.
- End the rape and plunder of the earth and its treasures in the interest of profit.

Are these principles frighteningly close to the words of our leaders? Are they terrifyingly close to the laws of our ancients?

On the flip side of the coin, I can well understand why Native people scorn leftist ideology in North America. They point to the white left, the myriad communist parties, their history of treachery against us, and ask me if I am out of my mind. (I wouldn't be surprised if the answer was a categorical yes, but I am no shrink so I am not going to answer that one directly.) All I can say is: I know how it feels to be truly alone. I do not accede to their lusting after our homelands. I know how they are. The white left in this country seeks to remake us, to wrest control of the country from their own enemy and divide the spoils among themselves. Obviously, no Native person could agree with that.

The subject of the development of the left, its history of betrayal of Native people, is not for this work. I intend to treat this subject very seriously elsewhere in another work. Herein, I wish to paint my own life in all its complexity. The side of Native people most impossible for the left to deal with centres on our concept of "spirituality." Not surprisingly, we ourselves find it difficult to grasp.

It must be borne in mind that the left in CanAmerica is predominantly white and male. These leftists have traditionally pooh-poohed that which is, for them, inexplicable. Along with sexism/racism, there is dogmatism. Being a white leftist in CanAmerica is tantamount to joining the holy church of Karl Marx, the atheist. If that is contradictory and confusing, never mind; you have just experienced the illogic of the middle class —confusion is their general state of mind. Being an atheist does not mean that we ignore the very phenomenon which defines all things—spirit, essence. To possess a spirit is to be alive. It does mean that we strip spirit of its mystical cloak and look at it in the cold light of reality.

To acknowledge the existence of spirit, to say that it is spirit that defines a living thing, to say that spirit is the motive force governing every living thing is not equal to a belief in a Great Spirit, Supreme Being or God. To define Indian-ness, Native culture, through belief in monotheism or a Great Spirit deity, is to blind yourself and confine all others to the narrow parameters of your own vision.

The body of a person in its death-state shrinks. From life to death, a person loses six or eight unaccounted-for pounds. I am no scientist, but logic tells me that the spirit has mass and weight. Science has not yet unravelled the mystery of the spirit; thus, no dollars are allocated to such research. This does not negate spirit's existence, it only shrouds it in mystery.

"I hear my grandmothers speak" is one remark which brings

either howls of laughter or nervous looks of skepticism from the faces of most atheists and even Christians. Psychiatry is predicated on dispelling the delusions of patients who hear voices. The victims of voices are influenced by the notion that hearing voices is connected to insanity or religious fervour. Some of them even take on the behaviour patterns of religious fanatics or mental derangement, or so psychiatrists maintain.

Sound travels in waves. It is transmitted by electricity. The body possesses an electrical system on which it operates. When you fast and drink water, you alter your electrolyte balance. Is it possible that the body can, through the ceremony of sweats and fasting, transform the electrical balance of the body in favour of reception rather than transmission?

Sound waves do not leave the earth's atmosphere. They remain caught forever in the atmosphere. The living voices of the dead remain trapped in the air we breathe and travel on the wings of their own waves. Again, I am no scientist and do not intend to unravel this very sticky and complex problem, but if spirit and holy knowledge exist, then they must have a basis for their existence in science. It must be possible to explain spirituality in scientific terms.

Science means to know. It implies rational knowledge. Rational thought has its foundations in mathematics, which since the industrial revolution has limited the type of knowledge considered reasonable. I am afraid science knows very little of itself. To answer questions with nebulous phrases or to dismiss them because our concept of knowledge is restricted to mathematics is to remain ignorant.

It is just a little narcissistic for Native people to say that we always were a spiritual people, as though others were not. Everyone has a spirit; whether or not she reconciles herself to her spirit or strives to understand it does not change the fact of its existence.

What is often attributed to creativity, I believe is more properly connected to spirit. Most poets agree. They will go to great lengths to achieve the inspiration necessary to write. Spiritualism is not a learned or bequeathed gift. It is natural to us all. It can, however, be obstructed and even crushed. It can also be harnessed. A person can be taught to reject its vitality. She or he can be prevented from making use of its potential. But spirit cannot be handed out. Only death causes spirit to depart from the body. "Indian doctoring" is the harnessing of spiritual energy. Our healing process is based on the assumption that illness, dis-ease, is inside the body. The whole of the body is ill. Healing will be done primarily through the spirit. Spirit and body join together against the illness. What Native medicine does is harness the reserve of spiritual strength to assist the body in purifying itself of the disease. All the methods of healing that Native doctors use are directed at purification. This makes sense if one considers that the major cause of disease is the presence of toxins and foreign bodies in the body.

I find it hard to believe that our people prayed before the days of conquest. To pray means "to beg, plead, beseech." It is my understanding that begging was against our ancient laws. Prayer is not synonymous with ceremony. Spiritual healing is referred to by many Native doctors as "putting our minds together to heal." That is not the equivalent of prayer. However, there is no word for this process in the English language. We then must make one up or integrate our own word into the language.

English does not express the process of ceremony. Yet, we are forced to communicate within its limits. We must differentiate and define our sense of spirituality in English.

I am going to defy orthodox science in the European sense, Marxism in every sense, and some of our own people whose spiritualism is limited to monotheistic prayer. I have no interest in being the scholar who researches the phenomenon of spiritual healing. I am not going to test its validity or even justify my experience with it. I will merely state that when I speak with my grandmothers before me, they answer. I do not believe in a Great Creator.

"Do you think we came from monkeys, then?" many people respond with contempt. Then they glance sideways and take note of my hairy arms. What that implies is that they were there when it all began and that there were only two possible ways by which we came into being: one, the Great Creator (a man, no less) made us, and two, monkeys became men.

I believe that creation is and will remain a mystery until I die. To have some guy come along and tell me that the whole of creation rests on a mythical male creator, or a male monkey, is just too narrow a range of options for me. I am not an impatient person. I can wait until I depart the earth before presuming that I know the answer. Until then, I content myself with repeating something one of our ancestors understood about Europeans: "White men are arrogant; they think that while still living they can solve the great mystery."

I think that white people who indulgently refer to us as a spiritual people are unable to escape the chains of a parasitic culture. Parasites need a host to sustain them. They cannot sustain themselves. White people do not produce the stuff of life for white folk. Even in their own land, the majority of farm labourers are non-whites or children. Since white adults rarely work at productive labour that is physical, they cannot conceive of laboriously unravelling their bodily person and discovering their spirit within. They gape at us in the hope that through the process of osmosis they will acquire some sense of spirituality.

We bare our spirit naked for them that they might ingest some of it. After having robbed us of land, wealth and livelihood, they now want our spirit. And we strive to give it to them. Well, I don't remember my grandmother ever telling me that there was any virtue in surrendering my spirit, so I don't.

For those white people who seek to discover their spiritual

being I say: fast, walk in the mountains or on the bald prairie, bathe in the rivers, eat only what nature provides, sweat and re-discover your spirit. There is no easy route to spiritual re-birth.

A man chooses
A woman
To join and share their lives
To bring new life
To strengthen his people

A man chooses
A path
Following the old laws
Set in today's world
To free his people

Respect and honour your wife
Your actions
Teach
This new life
Our children
Our future

DENNIS MARACLE

15. Pork Chops and Applesauce

SOME OF US honestly believe that since CanAmerica is rich, it is the centre of the universe. It produces great wealth. It is sad, but the truth is that CanAmerica is a consumer, not a producer, of wealth. It produces extremely little compared to what it consumes. Stop the flow of diamonds, gold, silver, foods, electronic gizmos, even cars, from other lands to the ports on our shores and you will see how rich this continent is, friends. Businessmen run this continent. They also own it. A smart businessman is one who can build his factory in South Africa, take advantage of the "jim crow" apartheid laws, extract the raw material from our home and Native lands (tax free), and spend his money in New York, Toronto, Vancouver or Montreal. He is brilliant if he spends his money on the stock exchange, "making" more money.

We see all this and from a distance it does look awesome. Totally. CanAmericans are the most fed, the biggest, the most affluent and the fattest people in the world. Their language reflects their opulence. General Motors "leads the world";

something else is the "finest product in the world." We listen to the ads on television and radio and we read the ads in magazines, on billboards and in newspapers and we buy them. At least some of us do.

These businessmen are the parasites that our Native leadership now worships and wishes to engage in joint corporate ventures with. In the end, it is business itself that will benefit from the tax breaks, and as poor urban Canadians the majority of us will suffer for another hundred years. Our history will be reduced to one of ritual, song and dance and our struggle turned into a puling cry for help. (Could it be that Black Americans are not the only ones that white people and their friends think have rhythm?)

My whole life is lived with the firm conviction that neither Canada nor the United States "belongs" to Europe. This land was wrested from us by force and since conquest (not "contact"), Europeans have built a system of lawless pillage and plunder of the earth and its people on the graves of our ancestors. Every time I say that people jump and cry, "What are you going to do with all these white people, send them back to Europe, drive them into the sea, put them onto reservations?" In their colonized minds they see their white spouses, victimized by a crazed amazon. You flatter me. As though I really could do any of these things.

All I can say is, I am not a beast. Europe has been the historic beast; to accuse me of bestiality stuns me. It hints of the sort of fate you may have in store for those who would rebel against the nature of this system. Could it be some of us are so filled with self-hate that we have delusions of running amuck among the rebels, shooting and killing at will, à la Pinochet of Chile? There are some Natives who weep and cry "Beast" whenever another Native dares to stand erect. These Natives know, you see, that the price that white people must pay for us to stand erect is for white people to stand on their own two feet and cease balancing

on our backs. We should stop being so proud of carrying a
shit-load of parasites on our backs.

Europeans in CanAmerica took our entire homeland and
gave us a welfare cheque. Not satisfied with that, they have the
brass to resent the piddling cheque we are given. I am not trying to justify welfare. It has not been good for us. But, let us
stop pointing fingers at the victim and challenge the thief. I am
told that all that is history, and that you cannot change history,
blah, blah, blah. And do you close your eyes at the scene of a
Native rising off her knees and envisage tanks rolling over her
and quake with fear? Do you imagine that the man might mistake her for you and roll over you too?

I am a hungry woman. I hunger for my homeland, ailing
and sick though it is. Ka-Nata, "spirit of community." I hunger
for an end to the robbery and for the spirit of community to
envelop my home again.

At sixteen, I hated these dog faces. I have changed. I no
longer hate them, but I am not a turn-the-other-cheek, jump-
on-the-bandwagon, fancy-assed "squaw" either. I am a pagan
woman with a deep and stubborn sense of justice and a hungry
spirit.

The worst of it is that they could not build this beast of prey
by their own labour. They pillaged Africa for Black hands to
build their colossus and they pillaged Asia for the skills and
knowledge necessary to transform the world. Their essence had
not changed. The land and its treasure is ours and the labour is
Black.

The land does not belong to Black people, but the fruit of
their labour does. They alone have earned their place in the
sun-dome of our future. Black people paid for this country with
blood, sweat and tears. To Black mother do I offer a piece of
CanAmerica, unconditionally, for she had to sacrifice so many
of her finest daughters. With her alone do I strike a partnership,
an equal right to re-build a nation more lovely than the settlers

can imagine. All others will have to fall in line or be left behind, outside the warm circles of our fires.

I am not insensitive to the plight of the early white immigrants. I know that your own people threw you into filthy, disease-ridden, ex-slave ships and sent you here, penniless. (Womanless, too.) I know that you were dumped here because your own countrymen did not want wretched paupers messing up their system. But, quite frankly, the persecution you suffered you perpetrated on me. That changes the terms of our alliance. My friendship with you is not unconditional.

You were the overseers of slaves for the same dishonourable businessmen who persecuted you. You were the head-hunters of scalps that the dishonourable businesses paid for. You will have to address that history, alter it and transform yourself in the process.

Now these "honourable" businessmen have called into being sacred Red bureaucrats to execute their system (and our rebels, if need be) for them. Is that why I occupy such a very large space in some of their minds? The cowards of the elite cannot deal with conflict openly. Instead, they indulge in vitriolic gossip to annihilate the opposition.

Do you think our relatives don't know how much we hate each other? Do you think that our folk don't see that your attacks on those who oppose the direction you take isn't part of this hate? Do I need to remind you of a little of our reality? Two years ago a three-month-old baby girl was raped by her father and died from it. He got five years in the "queen's hotel."

Four years ago a little girl told my cousin that she wanted to stay with her on weekends. My cousin asked her if her parents beat her up. It wasn't that. "Every Friday, my two brothers and my dad get drunk and make me screw them. I don't want to do it anymore. Do I have to?"

"Lee," my cousin cried, "this little twelve-year-old girl did not even know that she had the right to say no."

My daughter told me her friend would not be seeing her for a long while. She was out trick-or-treating and didn't tell her boyfriend or her grandma where she was going. Her dad knew where she was, but her boyfriend did not think to ask him. Her boyfriend called her aunt and her grandma and then he called the cops. Now her aunt is going to come and take her away from her dad. Her dad gave her money to run away to Seattle. My girl has no friend—again. She doesn't think about that, she thinks only of her friend, a motherless child who is not able to be with her dad. What are our thirteen-year-old girls doing with twenty-year-old boyfriends anyway?

Catholicism killed our mothers. Mary died giving birth to her nineteenth child, and because the State did not think fathers fit to rear babies, the child is fatherless as well.

"Does your boyfriend ever hit you?"
"Yeah."
"Don't you think it is not nice for a man to hit a woman?
"Well, he only does it when I'm bad. He worries about me a lot."
And my daughter sighed the sigh of an aged woman, despairing of a lost girl.

That we assist in our oppression does not make it right. That colonialism has been so thorough, so devastating as to convince our poor folk that we deserve this hard time does not make it right. To believe that all of us will continue down this path of national suicide forever is to live in a fool's paradise. One day, Man Friday will just decide to get hold of Crusoe's gun and shoot him.

In North America Native peoples possess the luxury of not having to resist colonialism—we resist each other. We do not possess the luxury of constituting the majority in our own land.

The majority in CanAmerica enjoy a standard of living that does not drive them to want change. They couldn't care less that the lives of Native peoples are threatened by the invisible prison we live in.

On Native Resistance

I have more in common with an African ex-slave
than my Mayan cousins of Guatemala.

In the Third World, Natives resist oppression.
In America, the Natives resist each other.

Our loyalty consists of our self-
        and mutual contempt.

The price of our loyalty:
a "farewell" cheque, once monthly.

I have stood in the meeting halls of the elite, articulated the fallacy of reducing our struggle for self-determination to a real-estate deal and been laughed at. Not to worry: loss of pork chops and applesauce will cure that. The same cure will work for the apathy of white people.

All of that has a practical application in life and I sometimes think that that is what men hate most about women. Women are too pragmatic and practical. If we think something, we will live our lives that way. If we think colonialism is bad, we will do whatever we can to end it. We women cannot be counted on to let hypocrisy go unnoticed. I am so weary of men who, guilt-ridden by their own treachery, attack me and accuse me of the very things they are bogged down with.

If I am against colonialism in particular, then I must also be against colonialism in general. That means that I resist the threat of invasion of El Salvador by the lunatic regime of Ronald Reagan and that I support the boycott of South Africa. "Until those Black people in South Africa can stand up, we're never going to get anywhere," Cj once said.

Azania

I saw you working in my sleep last night,
Azania
I saw you working in my sleep.

I saw you turning over stones
a baby on your back
I saw the urgency on your face
the futility, Azania
of forcing food from stone.

I saw you working in my sleep last night,
Azania
I saw you working in my sleep.

I saw your hands unload sulphur
from lands of mine, long gone
I saw the bitterness on your face
of unloading death, Azania.

I saw you working in my sleep last night,
Azania
I saw you working in my sleep.

This may seem strange to you
Azania
But for every dollar Cansulex
squeezes from your hungry hands
a million of us share a dime.

I saw you working in my sleep last night,
Azania
I saw you working in my sleep.

I saw those Natives of Ka–Nata
spewing from the plane
and I must say, I was not surprised.
You cannot see my desperation
at the hands of our Bantustan chiefs in Ka–Nata.

I saw you working in my sleep last night,
Azania
I saw you working in my sleep.

Between silk sheets
les couturiers de l'impérialisme
have decked out their puppets
Certainly, they are welcome in South Africa.

In the 1960s we wanted to dismember the empire. By the
'80s the empire had dismembered the movement. What is at the
heart of it all? There are solidarity movements for a growing
number of struggles led by expatriates living in Canada. There
has been the occasional attempt by a few intellectuals to rationalize the solidarity movement and establish closer co-ordina-
tion of the work through coalitions. But the solidarity movement remains disjointed and ineffective, in much the same way
that the peace movement and the ecology and Native movements are largely ununited.

Canadians have not sat down with themselves and asked,
"What do I want to do here? Am I in solidarity with this or that
because I actually want to effect change in the world? Am I
doing this because I disdain injustice in a country committing
crimes against its own people? What relationship does solidarity
activism have to me? Why am I doing this?"

The various groups, headed as they are by refugees and expatriates who dream of repatriation under a new social order, are unable to prioritize their activities in accordance with the strategic interests of the movement of people in Canada toward our emancipation. I would be disappointed if they did consider the interests of people here ahead of their own.

To promote self-interest among Canadians would have a lasting and damaging effect on Native people unless it were tied to a different consciousness, such as internationalism. Native participation should not, however, be governed by the interests of Canadians or the oppressed people we are supporting. Whatever decisions we make, must be made with the interest of our struggle at heart. This means that we participate and promote solidarity work, because until South Africa is liberated, we will always be the primitive younger brothers of every other race of people in the world. We are no longer the equal of any race of people but Blacks in America.

I am invited to everyone's soirée and demonstration because I can perform. It is likewise with my Black American counterparts. Lorde! The more things change, the more they remain the same. If South Africa is not free, I am never going to get off my knees.

There are so few Native people involved in the solidarity movement that those of us who are ought to get together and plan our involvement in our own interest. For us solidarity work is not a fad. It is a vital part of our survival. We had better hope that when South African Blacks raise a new flag of hope over South Africa, we are counted in the ranks of people who helped make it possible.

16. Normal vs. Natural

THE ABYSS OF internalized violence is very deep. We need to stop subjecting each other to violence and love each other more. Think of when a white woman in a supermarket makes a face, looks at your jacket suspiciously and then tallies the groceries. You know inside yourself that she thinks you stole something. Sometimes the cashier will even ask if you have enough money "to pay for all this." You save it. You just answer yes, withholding the rage you are feeling inside. You go home. Your kids are quarrelling and the old wooden spoon is trotted out and a licking handed down. My girl fought me as a six-year-old. The war got out of hand and I laid a dirty beating on her.

What the hell was I doing? I asked myself later. I gave to my child what I should have handed to the people who poured the rage down my throat. At twenty-five, I decided no more. The result has been tremendously liberating for all of us.

It is no different for middle-class Natives. White bureaucrats, government officials, etc., tell us we aren't ready for this or that. We are not qualified for this or that job. We nod agreement, go

home and talk about the compromise we had to make. This is
not compromise. Compromise, by definition, is two sides giving
up something in order to come closer together. What the
middle class is asking us to do is continue to make concessions.
Any more concessions and we will be falling down the abyss of
national suicide. If the State won't kill us, we'll have to kill ourselves.

Love is a practical matter. The mother who does not feed her
child or hear its cry in the night does not love that child, no
matter what she says. Talk is cheap and her actions scream the
truth. Likewise with men. If you are patient with white folk and
wale on me and my children, I know who you really love.

Our children need to know, more than anything else, that
their parents love each other. Instead of coming together, just
the opposite is happening. Half the Native children in Can-
America are raised without fathers! You were all there on conception day, so where did you go after that?

Mothers, we have to teach our children not to blind themselves to truth. Let's not pretend that all is well. Children do not
make good parents. If you don't know what to do, find an older
woman who does and talk to her. Our children need to feel that
they have some value to us and to themselves.

Our daughters need us to live. It is sad when the victims must
take responsibility for altering the conditions of their victimization, but that is reality. We are the people who are going to
change things around here and we cannot do that if we are
pointing fingers at ourselves and our children.

I heard a joke the other day. I laughed until I wept. Two men
are sitting on the dock at False Creek crab-fishing (a dubious
thing to do, given the state of the local waters in Vancouver).
One is an Indian and the other is white. The Indian sets his trap,
goes away and returns an hour later. He removes his trap and
hauls out a half-dozen crabs. The white guy sets his trap and an
hour later, pulls it out of the water. There is a single, lonely crab

in it. This scenario is repeated over and over. Finally, the white guy says, "What's going on, Indian? I set my trap right next to yours, use the same bait, and bingo, yours is full and mine has but one lousy crab." The Indian looks carefully into the white guy's bucket, studying his crabs. "Well, I can see at a glance, your crab is white and my crabs are Indian." "What the hell does that mean?" the confused man replies. "Well, I set my trap and my crab pulls the other crabs down with him."

This attitude travels to all levels in and outside the family. One need only repeat a rumour and all and sundry jump on the bandwagon. "Oh, I knew it." The rumour may come from the slimiest, most dishonest and unprincipled person, but we believe rumours even when they are obviously lies.

When white people don't have to give up anything and we are expected to compromise, that is called injustice. If we go along with it, it is called selling out. Who is going to pay for this? Our families. When that man comes home from the supermarket, his wife is going to say something less than perfect and because he needs to fight, her eyes are going to be black in places where they ought to be honey-brown. The one thing about human beings we can all be sure of, besides death, is imperfection. We don't need to goad each other to screw up. We do it naturally.

We have little pride in the face of white men, and no end to arrogance at home. It is time we turned that around. Let us show pride in front of white folk and be humble at home. If your home is filled with useless and harmful violence, then revolution will bring peace and tranquillity. Revolution is not always violent, but it is always the opposite of what has been.

Love is a thing of the spirit. Let us carefully nurture it with patience, tenderness and encouragement and not shame each other with violence.

If you can't stand me crying, then you can't face your own pain. If you think it is a crime for me to want recognition, then

you want me to remain invisible. If you don't know why you
have patience with white folk and rage for me, then you are not
looking in the mirror for affirmation.

If you truly want to understand spirit, you must stop thinking
in terms of normal and begin to understand what is natural.
White men would not be so obsessed with "normal" if they
could think about how the mothers of their nation waited on
them as little creatures. These moms struggled, day in and day
out, to teach them the basics of life. "No, you do not pee in
your bowl after you eat your cereal . . . No, I don't think it is a
good idea for you to wear the bowl on your head . . . Pardon
me, did you just tell me that you kicked your sister off the
porch? . . . Is that her I hear, still screaming?"

Some of the memories my children have left me are priceless.
Once we were in the local neighbourhood laundromat and Col
was barking, again. My husband said, "Don't you think we
ought to stop her?" His idea of parental guidance is to enforce a
multitude of prohibitions that no two-year-old could possibly
remember. "No." My response was a kind of calm catatonia. An
old Italian man who thought Col was cute petted her and she
bit him—hard. At his scream, we both popped our heads into
the dryer. We looked at each other and her dad said, "Don't you
think we ought to get her?" "Only if he hurts her."

I knew it was the wrong answer by the look on his face. I
don't need to tell you who went and got her, apologizing pro-
fusely to the old man. That is the sort of humbling that women
go through all the time. If I had punished my daughter, she
would have missed out on mastering her own spirit.

Fathers are shocked at some of the antics of their children.
Mothers often hide the details of their children's lives from their
partners. By the time the children are teenagers, the mother is
quite calm when junior brings home some of her reality. (That
is, she raised her child instead of dragging her up.) Mother tries
to calm father down, assure him that the kid is going to grow

up, and no tantrums from parents will stop her. We know, after all, that Columpa doesn't crawl around biting people anymore. As mothers, we dealt with it all.

There is nothing normal about having a child. Procreation is natural, but it is not normal. It is a bloody revolution carried out with much pain, labour and blood. After nine months of co-habiting the same body, mother and child set to work one day, pushing, pulling and tearing at the body so the child may escape the dark womb. The womb that was safety and security to that child will open up and eject a helpless child. A woman's body will have to transform itself, instantly as it were, from an enclosed cage to an open canal. Volunteering yourself up for such pain is not normal.

Birth is a bloody beginning for both mother and child. Children try their mothers' patience continuously from birth. The reward is that you will have all these embarrassing memories that you can lay on your children when they start to get too big for their britches. The advantage that mothers have over everyone in their lives is that they know their family better than the family knows itself. The family has little idea who mother is.

We are patient, amused and delighted by slow and steady progress. Even the brightest three-year-old is an intellectual midget, yet I have endured philosophical discourses about life, death, growing up and growing old from a half-dozen three-year-olds and enjoyed each one.

About age three is when the colleagues of your little daycare attendee note she is brown. They mention it to her. "Well," she relates to me, "I tol'dem, dat everyone is born white, but some of dem get to be brown 'cause they are more beautiful. *And,* if they're really beautiful, den dey turn black, right Mommy?"

If you can listen to that without laughing, figure out how she arrived at the conclusion and realize that she has strung together a number of things—unrelated things—in an attempt to rationalize the relationship between race, consciousness and beauty, then you are a great woman, even if you are a man. Don't get me wrong. I know that not all women are able to do the above. It is just that the few people who are able to think quickly, control their basic urges and understand children, happen to be women.

If you want to understand what it takes to grasp spirit and harness its great energy reserve, mother a child. Don't father one. There are a lot of single dads around who are great fathers, but they are fathers, not mothers.

Let me tell you about dads. The best dads don't give up a damned thing in the interest of their children. They want something, they get it. Mother will manage to find a way to make up the difference. They want to do something, they do it. And when they are saddled with the care of their own children, they refer to it as baby-sitting!

Women give up things to rear children. I have given up friends because they said, "Sure come over, but, ah, don't bring the kids." I bought my first kitchen table after some thirty-five years of living. I have seen women walk about with tattered coats and torn shoes because the children needed braces. I have heard dads object to cosmetic teeth correction.

You stay home. You cook. You work, take the kids to day-care, then go home and cook. You clean and you care, when it hurts to care, but somehow you manage to reach inside and care some more. You watch. You watch and think about these little human beings that hardly resemble accomplished people. You have great faith that someday they will make it. You watch and ask, "Is that depression on my son's face? What is bothering him? Why are those two girls fighting all the time?"

The much-written-about phenomenon of sibling rivalry is considered normal by white male experts on child-rearing. To me, it is a threat to the collective unity that a family ought to represent. Rivalry between peers is never healthy. Brothers and sisters will live some thirty or so years after their parents have gone, if things go right. They will need each other one day. It is no test of positive behaviour for children to treat adults with respect. Children are much more cognizant of the power structure inherent in a family than adults admit. If they are good to their peers, it is a real mark of virtue. Children are aware that the power relations between them are very different.

When the neighbour comes and cusses out your child, you tell him where to go. Your child is not an animal. You chuckle after the altercation is over, go inside the house and ask your son if he really did piss in that guy's underground parking lot. If you have a "normal" husband, likely he was hiding in the kitchen. His normal reaction to your mixing it up with the neighbour is to instruct you to be polite—less aggressive.

For a Native child to grow up and take this world on in the way that she will have to to survive, she is going to have to be tough, brilliant and well loved. Self-reliant would not hurt either. At the least, we have to be determined. Men not only do not see this, they do not even think about such things until the child is already halfway out the door and ready to hit the streets in search of work and an independent life.

No one actually told us straight out to blind ourselves to our sons. Perhaps one day at school a young boy was laughed at for caring and all the other boys, including our own, lined up behind the boys doing the laughing. Because sensitivity is not normally a boys' trait, our sons joined in the laughter. They did not look at or think about the things that would help their sensitivity to take root and grow. They ignored the world of agony around them and lost touch with themselves. We didn't see it happen.

It is the spirit that cannot be lied to. The spirit sees everything in its longevity and in its brevity. Since white men define the world in terms of norms, naturally they pooh-pooh and make fun of those of us with a little spiritual sight. "Seeing," our old people call it. Without an awakened and sharpened spirit, everyone's vision is going to be impaired. In general, CanAmericans, in particular white men, prefer looking at life with the drapes drawn.

For a defeated and demoralized people, it is understandable that the wherewithal to stand up for oneself will be lacking. I did not finish high school. I think about that all the time. In the flower of my youth, at my most vigorous and brightest best, I failed. This failure shades my audacity. I hesitate when applying for work. I have a hard time drawing up a resume and believing that I really did do everything written on its pages. Several members of my family did not finish high school—the majority, in fact. My daughters are going to have to attend an adult training facility like their mother and grandmother. At age fourteen they could not deal with the loneliness and alienation that high school spelled for them. A pall of grey, a mist of doubt, will follow them for a while.

This grey colours their spirit. To peel it back is a great fight with the self and the world around them. Layer upon layer of the ugly truth of this society will have to be peeled away for them to reconnect with the beautiful self within. Re-connecting with their grandmothers will provide them with the ancient strength to peel off the shades of grey encumbering the audacious, loving spirit.

Spirituality is re-connecting with the self and our ancestry. It is doing the right thing for your family and your community. Burn sage, brothers and sisters, but when you are burning it and carrying a small child, think about going to school and fighting red-neck teachers, the nicest of whom is going to ask you to erase yourself and be like him. Our kids need to know that we are on their side.

Loving children is one of the most difficult of life's tasks. It is one of the things that is very hard to do well. Procreation, pure and simple, is natural. But loving children is work, work for which there is no reward. When mothers ask where all the years went, they already know the answer and can't really grasp the magnitude of its simplicity. They were spent watching, fixing, making and cleaning. They were spent looking for shoes, buttoning buttons, doing up shoelaces, finding coats, cooking and comforting little children with big tears.

Men get some of that care. If your husband is wandering about quietly searching for something, you ask him what he is looking for, then you tell him where it is; all the while you pick up the baby, wipe her nose, put her down and turn over the eggs. But you don't miss what was happening outside the window, do you? "Look, so-and-so must have a new car." You bang more pots and pans and shuffle more things.

Someone saw my partner at a gathering and asked, "Where's Lee?" "She's over there, under a pile of kids." I didn't think about it then, but that was how he saw me for some time. For a long time I used to think it must be hard for him. Most of the children were not his. Hard for him? I raised three of my own, his, and helped with a host of others with skill and grace. My children will tell you it was with love and both eyes open. All parents begin by loving their children. Skill and grace is what you apply to achieve understanding and learn to like them.

Love is what drives you to rise in the early hours of the morning, feed and clothe the kids and get them off to school before you go to work. Love stops you from beating the Jeezus out of the monster when she kicks her sister off the porch, pisses in the yard or paints the wall with a felt pen. Liking them takes much more work. It is hard to like a person as outrageous as that. It is not a given. The personality of this unknown quantity, when it finally takes shape, quite independently of you, may not be what you bargained for. You get what you get. You can't return the damaged goods, or the aesthetically unpleasing child.

Labour is the watering hole for spiritual growth. There is no other way to experience your own spiritual development.

Labour
is a living thing

Bodily movement
an expression of life

Work,
beauty in itself

White men cannot stop thinking in terms of mathematical norms. It is not normal to kick your sister off the porch. It may be natural in the under-developed mind of a six-year-old, but it is not normal in the everyday world of adults. It is not normal to cry about something you cannot define. It may be natural for a child who lacks words to express emotions that way, but it is not normal.

Native women and some Native men know full well that what is abnormal is very often natural. Internalized racism is the natural response to the unnatural condition of racism. Likewise is hating the perpetrators of racism. We live with this truth every day. If you really want to know the difference between white male perception and everyone else's, it can best be summed up as the difference between normal and natural.

One is based on a mathematical formula and is completely divorced from any sense of humanity. The other is born of the natural world and is dependent on humanity for its definition. Nothing more on white men need be said.

17. The Women's Movement

A GOOD NUMBER OF non-white women have addressed the women's movement and decried the fact that we are outside the women's movement. I have never felt outside of that movement, except when I denied my own womanhood during my misguided youth. White women can hardly be expected to take responsibility for that. But then, I have never felt that the women's movement was centred or defined by women here in North America.

That the white women of North America are racist and that they define the movement in accordance with their own narrow perspective should not surprise us. White people define everything in terms of their own people, and then very magnanimously open the door to a select number of others. They let us in the door as we prove ourselves to be civilized. Such is the nature of racism. If we don't escape learning it, can we expect that they should?

We are part of a global movement of women in the world, struggling for emancipation. Women worldwide will define the movement, and we are among them. Until white women can come to us on our own terms, we ought to leave the door closed. Do we really want to be a part of a movement that sees the majority as the periphery and the minority as the centre?

I heard a white woman the other day talk about herself as a lesbian and refer to non-white women as minorities. That is the madness, the psychosis, of racism; the mistress accords herself distinction as a certain type of woman while erasing the womanhood of other peoples. For me, Audre Lorde most properly represents the women's movement in North America. The women's movement is all about the liberation of humanity from the yoke of domination. It is all about the fight against racism and sexism and their effects on our consciousness, no matter what colour we are. It is all about the struggle for unity between oppressed women and men.

There are some white women who truly wish to struggle with the effect that racism has had on their consciousness. That puts them at my doorstep, around my kitchen table. It does not inspire me to enter the master's wife's home, thank you very much. I do not have to urge white women to deal with their racism. The emancipation of non-white women of the world is taking care of that. The red-neck practices of the so-called feminist movement are already becoming history in some circles.

Some women accuse me of being angry and bitterly resentful about the life that this society handed me. You miss the real point. I write about racism to free my mind. Racism is the poison that crippled my tree. It also bent yours in all kinds of crazy directions. A talk, an intimate talk, between an ex-racist and an ex-victim of racism is not apt to be pretty.

Sojourner Truth told you already, "Ain't I a woman?" She asked the white feminist movement on our behalf, a hundred years ago, and the white women of North America have yet to face the answer. She served up the question; we need do no more.

The world is a dark world. It is an impoverished world. It is a world fighting for its survival. It is not concerned about Can-

America's definition of "women's issues." It is a world at war. Sojourner Truth properly reflects the world of today.

The women of the world are re-writing history with their bodies. White women of CanAmerica are a footnote to it all. I am not in the habit of concerning myself with footnotes. I am concerned about us, though. White women figure too largely in our minds. Let us stop chasing them and challenging their humanity at every turn. Let us begin by talking to each other about ourselves. Let us cleanse the dirty shack that racism left us. Let us deal with our men–folk and the refuse of patriarchy they borrowed from white men.

I represent the future of women in North America, just as any other woman does. That white women only want to hear from me as a Native and not as a voice in the women's movement is their loss. Embodied in my truth is the brilliance of hundreds of Native women who faced the worst that CanAmerica had to offer and dealt with it. Embodied in my brilliance is the great sea of knowledge that it took to overcome the paralysis of a colonized mind. I did not come to this clearing alone. Hundreds walked alongside me—Black, Asian and Native women whose tide of knowledge was bestowed upon me are the key to every CanAmerican's emancipation.

Audre Lorde and I were destined to be close. The combined knowledge of African ex-slaves and colonized Natives in North America is going to tear asunder the holy citadel of patriarchy. Who can understand the pain of this land better than a Native woman? Who can understand the oppression that capitalism metes out to working people better than a Black woman?

The road to freedom is paved with the intimate knowledge of the oppressed.

Perseverance

There's a dandelion on the roadside in Toronto.
Its leaves a dishevelled mix of green and brown.
    A dandelion scraggling 'n' limping along.

There's a flower beside a concrete stump
on Bay Street, in Toronto. Perpetually rebellin'
    against spiked heels and blue serge suits.

The monetary march-past of 5 o'clock Bay Street
(deaf to the cries of this thin aging lion)
    sneers: "Chicken-yellow flower . . ."

My leaves, my face . . . my skin . . . I feel like
my skin is being scraped off me. There is
    a flower in Toronto. On the roadside

It takes jackhammers and brutish machines to rip
the concrete from the sidewalks in Toronto
    to beautify the city of blue serge suits

But for this dandy lion, it takes but a seed,
a little acid rain, a whole lot of fight and a
    Black desire to limp along and scraggle forward

    There is a flower.

18. Flowers

I WANT YOU TO know why I love plants and their flowers. A writer looks for analogous things in her life, symbols to gentle or beautify reality. For me, people are like flowers. Some, like the dandelion, are plain but have a multiplicity about them that makes them valuable. A few are lovely parasites, sucking up more nutrients from the soil than is their share. No matter how plain or pragmatic, every flower has its own beauty, its miracle of artistry and extraordinary colour. Likewise with people.

Some flowers are not merely beautiful but highly specialized—extraordinary in their specialization. They are fine, sensitive creatures which bring light and joy to all. Others, like the nasturtium, are not so beautiful but are much sturdier and have a very long flowering time. Step on them and they carry on blooming. Waterless, they still grow. They bloom best in the midst of others.

We are right now in the autumn of our history. We are, as a people, a perishing lot. Unlike for the flowers, spring has not

rolled around for us for a long time. It seems the winter of our
life will never end. It is very hard for us to see and love the
colours of the flowers in spring.

"You have your writing to keep you alive. What have ordinary Native women got?" my friend asked. Right now, they
have nothing to ease the pain of a long autumn but their
courage to face a winter of struggle in preparation for re-birth
in spring. Our great blossoming is coming and we will bloom
bright, extraordinary, and the world will witness our unfolding.

Poets are like the perennial forget-me-nots that grew in my
sister's garden in the woods: rarely appreciated, except by those
with artistry in their lives. They never seem to die and they
never receive the accolades which roses get. It is sad and unfor-
tunate that women who take the time to plant and nurture
flowers cannot find comfort in their artistry. Some of the most
talented artists I know hide behind the pragmatic details of their
lives. They fear the death inherent in the cold and solitary winter that artists must endure.

I am a sturdy little flower, fearing nothing, including death.
Being perennial helps, though it has not made my life easy.
Being a poet has forced me to watch death with compassion and
an eye for detail. I look under stones for my own agony and the
agony of others. I sought writing as a means to expunge myself
of the misery I had worked so hard to collect. Perhaps that is
slightly masochistic, but so are forget-me-nots. What other
flower are people unabashedly cheeky enough to sit on?

People laud poets and painters and other literati as the roses
of their lives. Artists strive to capture the beauty of the rose. It is
never a self-portrait. If they ever manage to achieve real artistry,
they are immortalized. I don't know that I ever will be. I am not
sure I have that sort of devotion. It is the process of collection
and articulation that I love.

Last Words

NOT ALL THE READERS who picked up this book will have made it to the end. Those of you who did can content yourself with having gotten an inside look at the madness which the colonial process creates. The anger written on these blank pages has its origins in facing the reality of our bleak circumstances. I hope that my writing has not made you more depressed than you already were.

A Native man once told a group of writers that we shouldn't write about anger and sadness. He mentioned that angry books and sad stories full of hate sell to white folks. "They love it when we are fighting and hating each other." He mentioned Alice Walker's writing as an example. He seemed even more cynical than I sometimes feel. I doubt very much that he is one of the readers who made it to the end. There is little humour, little joy on these pages, but I am not so cynical as to believe that white people are going to happily plough through the pages which chronicle the devastation that colonialism has been in the chapters of our lives. And I don't believe Walker's book *The Color Purple* was a sad story full of hate.

ABOUT THE AUTHOR

LEE MARACLE is a member of the Stoh:lo Nation of British Columbia. She currently works as a partner in Native Futures Group, where she integrates her traditional Indigenous teachings with her European education to create culturally appropriate processes of healing for Native people. She has been employed by various First Nations groups and governments to teach general health seminars from a traditional perspective and to reclaim culture, sociology, law and government through language, creative writing and counselling. She is the Aboriginal "Mentor in Residence" at the University of Toronto, an award-winning teacher and the Traditional Cultural Director at the Centre for Indigenous Theatre.

Press Gang Publishers is committed to producing quality books with social and literary merit. We give priority to Canadian women's work and include writing by lesbians and by women from diverse cultural and class backgrounds. Our list features vital and provocative fiction, poetry and non-fiction.